International Political & Environmental Folly

Issue 8

by

Daniel Tissington

Published by New Generation Publishing in 2020

Edition 8

First edition published 2011

Issue 2 published 2015

Edition 3 July 2015

Edition 4 Published April 2016

Edition 5 Published June 2017

Edition 6 Published July 2018

Edition 7 Published January 2019

ISBN 978-1-80031-717-8

www.newgeneration-publishing.com

 New Generation Publishing

Notes on these seven Editions

Actions of individuals printed in Edition 1 , Edition 2, & Edition 3 are taken from previous printed Media Reports.

Edition 2 has added five paragraphs to the end of Chapter 8 and Reference 18 in the Appendix.

Edition 3 adds infortmation to the end of Chapter 5 & Chapter 8 of Issue 2

Edition 4 & 5 adds Information to the end of Chapter 5

Edition 5 also adds new information to end of Chapter 8

Edition 6 adds information to end of Chapter 5

Edition 7 adds information to end of Chapter 5

Edition 8 adds information to the end of Chapter 5

Contents

Title i

Disclaimers and Copyright ii

Notes on this Edition iii

Contents iv

Preface v

1 Introduction to the work 1

2 Introduction to Climate Changes 5

3 Global Warming 8

4 Triggering an Ice Age 12

5 The cause of 'The Big Bang' 14

6 Navigating our Globe through Space 20

7 Population Growth and Levels 23

8 Introduction to Political Shortcomings 27

9 More Political Shortcomings 33

10 Continuation of Political Shortcomings............................37

11 Analysis, Conclusions and Solutions................................43

Appendix...47

PREFACE

This work consists of eleven chapters which outline an expanded philosophy by extending ideas previously set down in an earlier work entitled 'Classical Environmental Folly' Edition 5, dated September 1992 (See Ref 4, Attached). This earlier work considered matters concerning the survival of the human species while exploring our relationship with and our dependency on the environment and vice versa. Appended to this work are fifteen [seventeen were intended] references that enlarge the overall perspective for the reader who has the time available and sufficient curiosity to delve deeper into the revelations this book exposes.

It seems that excessive extraction of food for human consumption and fuel for power and heating supplies from the Earth's crust and seas have not been given sufficient serious thought, and it is apparent that factors governing this plunder are being ignored world-wide for one reason or another. Resultant pollution is not being properly dealt with, indeed, some of it cannot be dealt with. In fact we, the human population, are living beyond the means of our planet and are draining and wasting resources unnecessarily. This 'excess' is evident without taking into account the consequences of climate changes which are cyclic and have been in operation for aeons of time - these changes occur with or without human populations or meddling politicians, who frequently seem to interpret these problems from a perspective that suits their own policies whereby they can needlessly increase taxation.

The author has now formulated a logical explanation as to the causes of climate change cycles, which include the oft-repeated cyclic occurrences of global warming, ice ages and, separately, 'the big bang'. With this understanding it is not inconceivable that, in the foreseeable future, humankind may be able to develop an 'engine' that employs the principles of the 'big bang' which, with proper development, might enable Mother Earth to be 'moved' from its present Solar Orbit and help avoid the consequences of a future 'black hole' or 'big bang' or an exhausted Sun star. Such a programme, properly executed, would enable our Earth to continue to provide a good and fruitful home for humanity for an extended period by replacing the existing sun that we live by in today's environment with another 'Sun star'! The foregoing maybe termed as 'Societies' Ill- Considered Problems'.

There are three overriding causes of 'Societies' Ill-Considered Problems':

1) CYCLIC CLIMATIC CHANGES INCLUDING THE 'BIG BANG'

2) HUMANITY FULFILLING NATURE'S REQUIREMENTS

3) POLITICAL SHORTCOMINGS

These three key points are expanded below.

1) There are many things that we, the human population, can do to negate or minimise the harsh consequences of ignoring the complete cycle change, which Mother Earth will experience if left to present day policies of our Leaders.

The complete cycle change is defined as occurrences from 'big bang To big bang'. But our 'Political Masters, some of whom seem to have 'the bit'* between their teeth', do not seem to understand the unstoppable causes of repeated Global Warming and Ice Ages, let alone prepare for them, and the inevitable tragedy for humans that these events will inflict. Furthermore, the event of the 'Big Bang' seems to be ignored by 'Our Masters' as something that might have emerged from a fairytale and this short-sighted perspective is indeed concerning!

* A 'bit' is an accoutrement that is used to exert pressure on a horse's fleshy mouthpiece and which is used to exercise control of the animal's movements when the animal is operating in a working harness

2) Population growth, which seems to be caused by Nature's subtle programming of all living species, including humans, coupled with political neglect/naivety of the problem.

3) Most Governments are facilitating the plunder of OUR planet by imposing excessive & growing tax levels - some of which appear fraudulent - coupled with unnecessary and illfounded legislation, thereby separately creating suitable conditions for extra population growth.

Bearing these key points in mind, the purpose of this book is to set out the programme and causes of the complete climatic change; that is from 'Big Bang to Big Bang'. Once we have a clear understanding of what drives climatic change, the text will include an explanation of humanity's contribution to the impending disaster by outlining the rationale behind the statement of 'humanity fulfilling nature's requirements'. The focus will then change to further explain the meaning of 'political shortcomings' and the consequences of this failing.

The foregoing will set the scene to enable informed analysis, conclusions and possible solutions to be penned.

The reader will then be able to decide if there is substance to the work and whether to persuade our 'Governors' to correct their unacceptable ways by refusing to vote for candidates who will not agree to adhere to the given path. It will not be an easy task because ' many of our Governors' think they know best and are not usually given to explaining their aims or reasons for their actions. Furthermore, they rarely give their constituents any say in matters which is a vital ingredient to long-term contented survival, an aim which may require us, the ordinary people, to reject 'GLOBALISATION' and endeavour to remain as individual Nations.

ONE
Introduction to the work

Although completely unaware of the fact at the time, the origins of this work really began in 1959 when the author returned home after two and a half year stint spent in Canada. Eighteen months of this period was in the Canadian Arctic, on the Islands north of the Canadian Mainland, and involved complex electronic defence equipment during which time he experienced 24 hours of continuous sunlight followed routinely by 24 hours of continuous darkness, together with temperatures falling to 53 degrees below zero. In all, a very worthwhile experience.

On returning to England a house was purchased with the intention of settling down to family life. At the time, in 1959, a reasonable house in a reasonable location could be bought for about £4,000 sterling and its Rate Demand (Local Authority: LA Tax) would have been about £25 sterling per annum, a sum which included sewage and often water services too. But the luxury of settling down didn't present itself. It may well have been possible if one had adopted the attitude of 'Yes Sir, No Sir. Three Bags Full Sir. Sorry About That and How Much Do I owe You?' This 'stance' was not really an option for the author. The LAs had been given too much power over private property, power which they often misused and still enjoy in increasing amounts to this very day.

The stark TV images of starving Nigerians suffering from the effects of famine finally stirred the initial intention of growing some vegetables into action, without, it has to be said, any previous experience of growing food. Now one may applaud or sneer at anyone growing vegetables, but if one owns a piece of land, it is a humble and worthy cause (particularly with the state of food supplies being what they are, rather than what they appear to be)...and it's clear that anyone stealing God-given sunshine with untended or misplaced forest trees in a residential area is being anti social and non- cooperative to say the very least.

The author naively thought that digging a piece of ground and planting seeds was all that was necessary to succeed with growing fruit and vegetables. However, the seeds did not germinate and it slowly dawned that the missing element might be sunlight. The rear garden was severely shaded by forest trees, on three sides! The wood at the bottom of the garden was the main problem at that time and the owners kindly gave permission to cut back the encroaching foliage and fell the offending trees. They also revealed the trees were protected by a recently applied Tree Preservation Order. [TPO]. This course of action started a ten year battle between the Local Authority (LA) who controlled the TPO, and the Writer's actions. As a result of this sun block, the garden soil and nearly all the plant life therein was diseased or stunted. In reality, this garden was vandalised by the LA's implementation of a TPO, and the author found that there are people who seem to get pleasure from ruining other people's gardens in this way.

Although Parliament has tinkered with this matter it still has not adequately dealt with it. The latest attempt to resolve this anti-social and yob type behaviour was to grant some control over the height of neighbouring Leyland ii tree growth, but this control is not only inadequate (and expensive) but lays in the hands of the LAs which caused the ten years of vandalism and heartache already mentioned. It should be clear that if one wishes to grow a rain forest then one must surely acquire a Continent to contain it, and if the forest happens to back onto a neighbour's land care should be taken to ensure that it cannot damage the neighbour's rightful use & enjoyment of their garden. However, we will return to the more detailed discussion on trees in much greater depth later, in the appropriate section of this book.

At the same time that the battle over the implementation of the TPO was being waged, the Local Authority was steeply increasing its local tax demands. This imposition was fought with great vigour but without success and involved Resident's Association Chairmen, Councillors, MPs, Ministers, Prime Ministers, The Queen of England, the Fraud Squad, and the Media to a limited extent. It seems as though increased taxation and the 'double charging' that went with the increases were approved by those approached for help in combating these outrages. The more tax Central Government allowed Local Government to demand, the more bureaucratic things seemed to get.

Finally, the most recent outrage allows the LA to seize private property that has been empty for longer than six months, renovate it if necessary, pass the cost onto 'the owner' and rent the property out to who-so-ever for a period of seven years. Oh, and the LA keeps the rent obtained for the use of the property. One could ask the MPs and Ministers responsible for this 'treachery' why the power over privately owned assets has shifted to LA officialdom. The level of Local Tax (now termed Council Tax) is 'banded' & based on the value of the property involved. Why is this so, you may well ask? Officialdom has no equity in privately owned property irrespective of powers granted by our 'Masters' or the beliefs that these legalised plunderers seem to hold. Tax demands, which includes ALL tax demands, should only reflect carefully controlled or minimised costs relating to essential services alone, unless the public accept a reduced status which includes serving as 'STATE SLAVES!' These increased costs, caused by taxation, are 'overheads' and mean the man in the street foregoes earned entitlements in order to pay for Government waste and abuse of power. It is time for Parliament to show some respect to those they represent and their assets. It should be noted that these particular, and other, increasing overheads are officially approaching 50% of GNP - the author thinks it is more than 50% - in this over-regulated land of Great Britain. Furthermore, these costs adversely affect GB's ability to maintain a healthy production of manufactured goods because we cannot compete with the emerging third world costs. Hence, for example, we are experiencing the loss of manufacturing ability of items such as motor vehicles and domestic electronics such as TV and so forth.

The author and a band of like-minded supporters formed a group called the Planning Acts Reform Committee (PARC), which recorded details of nonsensical and damaging planning decisions made under the rules of the Town and Country Planning Acts and raised these with the authorities, in the hope that a certain logic could be restored. Although the Act has been tinkered with by various administrations, it is fundamentally flawed, since you cannot sensibly (or morally) delegate non ownership authority of any privately owned asset. The results are ruinous....and this applies to nationhood also. The old adage that a man cannot serve two masters may be very apt when we consider the current situation with regard to Local Authorities, County Councils, Westminster and the EU!

So how come our elected individuals are freely giving away these powers of ownership to LAs and sovereignty to the EU? It doesn't, as is claimed for the case of the EU, even stop wars - there have been a series of serious skirmishes throughout the fifty odd years of the EU existence. And wars will always occur with or without 'globalisation' when a nation's fundamental existence is threatened. But never in the recorded annals of history has sovereignty been given away by Chieftains, Monarchs or Government Officials without the application of force and this is not required. Furthermore, unless this nonsense is brought to a halt, this unauthorised treachery will result in the relegation of this once Great Nation. The author terms the 'surrender' of these rights to the EU as 'unauthorised' since they appear largely be the results of the kind of actions displayed by our senior political leaders that should have been subject to Parliamentary approval.

I will never forget the plight of one old couple who found that their property was abruptly subject to flooding after a builder was given planning permission to build a new housing estate nearby. In spite of PARC's best efforts, councillors, planning officials or the builder* were never made to take responsibility for their vandalising decision or actions. This matter will be expanded later in the appropriate chapter(s), but at least now the reader has been given a glimpse of the origins of this work.

* It should be understood that the hammering given to elected bodies, bureaucrats and the system appear to be justified.....but at the same time there are some very helpful MP's Councillors and Public Servants operating in a very acceptable way. But fair minded elected representatives and state servants appear to be the exception rather than the rule!

For the record, a similar house to the one described at the beginning of this chapter would now cost some £400,000 sterling and its 'outgoings' would be about £2,000 sterling per annum. 'Outgoings' is quoted in place of tax because the LAs appear to have removed sewage, and in some cases water and other charges, from their demands and surrendered them to a third parties...but failed to reduce tax demands. The author has termed this inventive accounting practice 'double charging'. This recorded UK house price and local tax inflation has mainly been caused by the event and implication of The Town & Country Planning Acts, which, for a start, has caused a shortage of building land and has also created the useless need for hoards of costly bureaucrats.

Eventually the author retired to the South Coast where a report was issued to Parliament requesting Council Tax reductions (See Ref 8 Attached.) It showed a detailed account of 'Local Householder Outgoings' which had increased by 3600% over a period of some forty years accounting from 1959 for the South Coast Property against the RPI increase of 550%!

But, for now, we will endeavour to get to grips with causes of cyclic climate changes and the disaster these changes will inflict globally if a change of policy is not adopted by our politicians.

TWO

Introduction to Climate Changes

Since global climate change is cyclic, we have to break in to that circle somewhere and steadily work through the subject until we reach the point of the beginning again. So, since we are officially told that global warming is the current mode, let's look at what is thought to cause this phenomenon.

It may be prudent to point out that the last ice age occurred some 10,000 years ago when the glacier ice reached a latitude of about 50 degrees north i.e. viewed from the southern half of Britain, that would mean it spanned to the edges of London Town! The fact that glacier ice travelled that far south indicates there was a previous global warm period. It also shows that the ice came and went without the aid of people and their blamed greenhouse gas producing paraphernalia. But first we have to consider what causes the cycling to occur and why our globe fails to spin off into a colder and colder condition, or indeed, a hotter and hotter state. Especially when one realises that our sphere is orbiting the Sun star which radiates enormous amounts of energy and that our surroundings, i.e. outer space, is set at a very low temperatures indeed.

It should perhaps be pointed out that outer space is cold because the sun's emissions need to react with matter, such as air or dust, for example, in order to give off energy in the form of heat or light. And the fact that outer space is cold (and dark - look at the night sky) can be verified by observing the outside temperatures experienced by a passenger carrying aircraft at an altitude of say 50,000 feet where temperatures are around 50 degrees centigrade below zero, and greater altitudes suffer even lower temperatures.

Now, to appreciate the condition that the foregoing information imposes, we should turn our attention to lowering, and maintaining a fairly constant internal temperature of, say, a refrigerator. If we set the thermostat to a temperature somewhere below ambient temperature then we need a cooling device and a switch controlled by a sensor that turns the cooling mechanism on and off. But this switch must turn the cooling device on in the right condition, otherwise the refrigerator will end up getting colder and colder or get stuck at or near the ambient temperature.

For example, if the sensor that monitors the internal temperature of our fridge controls an electric switch which can turn the cooling mechanism to the 'on' or 'off' setting, this action must occur so that the cooling apparatus is switched on as the internal space of our domestic device starts to climb toward the ambient temperature. If the sensor switched the cooling device off at the previously stated juncture, then the fridge would just return to the ambient temperature, whatever that might be.

So the control of the mean temperature of our globe, which more or less supports life systems as we know them, has to be reacting to a properly 'sensed' control system. If the control system were improperly sensed to preserve a mean temperature, or the control exercised was random in nature then 'Sod's law' would ensure that the re occurrence of sequential global warming and ice ages would not, as they can be shown to do, occur, and we would not be here to debate the issue! NB We should recognise that life can only perpetuate where climate and other variables are cyclic or re-occurring, for example day following night, tides ebb and flow and seasons reoccur etc:. This occurrence is a chance issue, because nature is not concerned with the survival rate of any of its species, including humans. If a given species cannot cope, it becomes extinct. It may be that this last sentence needs to be emphasised and emphasised again, given the ramifications for all mankind. Now there is no doubting that the sun warms our planet and that this 'warming' experience is variable, according to season. This seasonal change is part of the 'steady as she goes' control of our mean temperatures. Seasonal control of our globe is caused by the tilt of the Earth's axis with respect to the centrally positioned sun. But the maintenance of the variation of the Earth's temperature to acceptable limits is enhanced by the heat content of the oceans. That is, Europe and South America are partially heated by circulating warm water produced by solar power in the shallows of the Caribbean and the Gulf of Mexico. European heat is carried by the surface water of the Gulf Stream across the Atlantic and northward towards Greenland and Iceland, where it eventually sheds sufficient heat to become dense enough to sink below the ocean's surface i.e. a given volume of water takes up less space when it is subjected to temperature loss and therefore becomes more dense or heavier per unit volume. This cold and submerged water then returns to the Caribbean and Gulf of Mexico to replenish its heat content plus the water taken from one ocean to another. In fact, our domestic central heating systems are a miniature replica of the Gulf Stream system!

Global warming, which is the current 'in' term of the modern politician, is cyclic and its gyrations are unstoppable. It is an aberration that interferes with the process of the system described in the preceding paragraph. King Canute of England knew better than this when his conniving courtiers are said to have told him he was so powerful he could control the tidal flow of the oceans. In order to teach his retinue a lesson, he sat on the seashore and commanded the sea not to wet his feet.

But our politicians have put limits and heavy taxes on carbon emissions in an attempt to cut the use of fossil fuels among the 'man in the street'. This is a vain attempt to stop global warming, or so they claim, but these rascals (I'm being kind) are kidding themselves at best and at worst are probably using the term to extract more taxes. They seem to be inflicted with the disease of the old '49ers', who were gold prospectors, suffering from 'gold fever' - translated, our politicians seem to have taxation on the brain, probably to provide income to keep them and their bureaucrats in conditions the rest of us can only dream about. How then, one wonders, do they explain away the tiers of extra and overpaid bureaucrats engaged to run 'their' over regulated regimes both locally and in Europe? These extra people not only mess our lives up administrating impossible regulations, but obtain massive rewards including huge salaries, inflation-proofed pensions and expenses for their unwanted and needless efforts, and all at our expense. But here comes the rest of quandary.

These people are able to maintain oversized properties, run up massive heating and lighting bills (in their home(s) and working environments), run 4x4s and maintain a luxurious lifestyle which adds massive amounts of CO_2 to our global situation - an occurrence our political 'Masters' say they are determined to reduce in order to stop global warming!

But the cyclic occurrences of global warming occurred long before man and his civilization existed. So the politicians current claim of prevention of global warming do not really seem to stand up to scrutiny... these political empire builders do not even bother to observe their own diktat and such behaviour needs exposing in the national interest. It maybe that they behave like this because they don't know any better, and it has to be said, politics offers the only high profile posts that can be obtained without proven ability or specific qualifications. They of course, answer to no one because, firstly, they grab 90% of the appropriately available microphone and camera times in order to declare their interest and make us aware of their efforts in countering global warming and, furthermore, the man in the street has become conditioned to accept the never-ending bunkum they dish out. Or perhaps he thinks protest is useless?

So we are left with the query: 'what exactly controls global warming?'

THREE
GLOBAL WARMING

The occurrence of global warming is caused by an aberration that interferes with the normal operation of the process as described in Chapter Two. The abnormality is caused by greenhouse gases such as CO_2, which encircle our globe at an altitude high above our heads.

These gases form a barrier to heat trying to escape from Earth but do not present the same barrier to emissions from the sun. It is only when heat re-radiates from Mother Earth, following a frequency change toward red end of the spectrum, that the gas acts as a barrier which effectively admits incoming solar energy and partially bars the passage of heat attempting to escape to space and, as a result, Earth's temperature increases. And this is evidently so because the polar ice-caps are melting or receding towards their respective poles. This 'frequency change' heat trap described in the preceding paragraph occurs in glass greenhouses also, and the cause of 'global warming, i.e. 'greenhouse gases' take the nomenclature from the greenhouses we use to persuade plants to grow out of season.

So we now have to ask how these gases get into the upper reaches of our atmosphere, if, as they have managed to do, and control the cyclic events that climate changes turn out to be, well before the event of mankind and his gas producing contraptions existed? Once again we have to look further afield to get the explanation that is now required. We also need to consider the various other theories that are said to cause global warming to occur. These need to be mentioned, whatever we think of them, because one of the auxiliary aims of this book is to get to the bottom of the subjects being examined in as much depth as possible. That is to clarify what we are facing and not to represent facts in a convenient manner like our politicians seem to do.

There is, of course, the official cause of global warming. It appears to blame the industrial and private use of carbon releasing fuels. But although these fuels obviously contribute something to the matter under discussion, the arguments put forward in this work seem to indicate that these occurrences are not the prime controlling events that some purport them to be. And then there are the emissions from humans and farm animals, which should be factored into our quest for answers. But these factors are not the cause of the cyclic pattern we have already shown exists. Likewise, with sunspots and Sir Fred Hoyle's belief that the switching from global warming to ice age, or the reverse, depends on the random presence of either electrically conductive or non-conducting particles which will switch climate traits by reflecting or admitting solar heating. It is worth repeating the apt statement made in Chapter Two: 'If the control system was improperly set to preserve a mean temperature, or the control exercised was random in nature then 'Sod's law' would ensure that the re occurrence of sequential global warming and ice ages would not occur as they can be shown to do and we would not be here to debate the issue!'

First of all then, in order to follow the proffered reasoning, we need to know where these gases emanate from, where they are stored and what happens to them prior to joining the 'blanket' that encircles our planet. The first of these storage mediums is found in dead molluscs or similar fish shells...relics that form the massive deposits of chalk found in the Chilterns and around our current sea shores: Dover and the Isle of Wight are well known examples of these gas-bearing materials. This particular 'store' is probably the most permanent of the known 'storage devices', but its storage ability is not necessarily permanent - a point we will return to later on. A second source of storage is fossil fuels such as gas, oil and coal. These deposits are said to emanate from dead plant life. Trees and other vegetation do act as temporary CO_2 storage devices until they come to the end of their time, at which point the gases are released.

There are also huge deposits of frozen or solid methane under, in, or 'atop' of the seabed. These accumulations of greenhouse gases are caused by bacteria operating on fallen leaves and branches of trees, which are washed down stream from tree-lined rivers banks. Methane gases are believed to exist in huge quantities - it has been said that there is enough to supply man's power needs for centuries. The gas, which is difficult to extract from the seabed, is also believed to burn cleaner than most other gas bearing fuels. (As an interesting aside, these gases are thought by some to cause the Bermuda Triangle mysteries.) The sun's rays are powerful enough to penetrate the depths of the seas and reach the seabed in this area of the world. The resultant warmth vaporises the solid blocks of cold and pressurised methane. This liberated gas naturally 'bubbles' its way to the surface, thus reducing the density of the surrounding waters. Bear in mind that a ship, or any other item, only floats if it can displace its own weight in water or other supporting medium before becoming submerged in the medium it inhabits. The result of this seawaters reduced density is that the ship sinks lower in the gaseous water in an attempt to restore its weight displacement. Since the ship is not designed to enable this endeavour, it sinks without trace. 'Without trace', because the disturbed seabed debris returns to the ocean floor after the event and completely buries the ship. On reaching the surface of the sea, these warmed gases rise.

Any low-flying aircraft passing over the area could easily cause an explosion with its hot exhaust pipe. So a low flying aircraft risks disintegration in this particular part of the world! Reports that aircraft navigational problems occur in this 'triangle' may be due to these rising methane gases being ionised. Such an occurrence might upset a compass reading, and although modern aircraft carry compasses, they usually fly at altitudes where such effects would be reduced by dilution of gas concentrates. Besides which, the main navigation reliance today is on directional radio beacons and GPS navigation. Assistance is usually available too, if needed, from ground based radar installations operated by Air Traffic Control.

However, methane gas has, in 2010, been reported by a scientific expedition as exuding in quantity from the Russian Arctic Tundra and the reported matter is probably duplicated in the Canadian Arctic. However, we must now get back on track! That requirement, before we carry on, also means indicating that we have just described unquantified natural sources of globally circulating 'green house' gas.

If we look at outcrops of rock that protrude from the earth's surface, we find that in many cases these protrusions are layered and the seams of these layers are not level with the horizon. They are in fact tilted at an angle of some 10 - 20 degrees to the horizontal. It looks as though these outcrops are emerging from the depths of the globe or sliding into the depths of the sphere. And in all probability some are going one way whilst others are going in the opposite direction. So what, we may ask, is causing these movements of matter?

Well gravity has something to do with the suspected movements. Gravity is almost certainly the prime source of power when we consider the reported movements of the Continental plates. And it is generally accepted that India's 'plate' has travelled from the American Continent and met with the Asian 'plate'. One of these 'plates' is generally thought to have slid over the other causing the Himalayas to come into being. Now, under these conditions, these plates are causing heat to be generated by the simple means of friction, and heat causes expansion of most materials, hence generated heat causes increased pressure of gases to occur. It also happen to be the case that pressure increases cause more heat to occur. One can check this out when inflating the inner tube of a bicycle tyre with a hand pump - the high pressure end of the pump gets quite hot. So in all probability, gravity and positive pressure have combined their various efforts to produce the said mountain range. There are also other agencies going through similar processes. For example, there is the globe's reported liquid iron-core to consider. Not surprisingly, it is claimed to be rotating at a different speed and direction to the surface of our sphere, and the resultant friction causes similar heat and pressure occurrences to the discussed 'plate' collisions. It is these internally generated pressures that cause outcrops of matter to occur and volcanoes to blow their tops.

So when a volcano erupts, it spews molten lava and gases from its base under the influence of positive pressure, and one cannot continuously take millions of tons of matter from any source without replacing it with a substitute! So where does this replacement material come from, we may well ask? Well, it is fairly clear that when a volcano 'blows its top' it has an enormous positive pressure driving its eruption, but as the matter being ejected slows due to a pressure drop, its temperature falls. And just as a rising pressure produces extra heat, the converse occurs with a falling pressure. Thus the lava flow comes to a halt and the exit hole in the volcano mostly seals with 'frozen lava'. However, matters don't rest there.

The falling pressure chills the remaining material and the earth's internal pressure falls even further. So we are left with a partial vacuum, the resultant force combines with gravity to 'suck in' any poorly secured material, including chalk, fossil fuel, methane and any other material that happens to be in the vicinity. Furthermore, when the next volcanic eruption occurs, some of this material, along with any greenhouse gas, will be ejected to cause or commence a global warming period.

It should be pointed out that there is a difference between the amount of crudely produced greenhouse gases spewed from a volcano or seabed and the minimised production of 'greenhouse gases' ejected from man-made devices which are scientifically designed to produce maximum power or heat and minimum amounts of greenhouse gases. In the case of the auto mobile, there are catalytic converters in use which further refine the exhaust emissions from an engine burning petrol for example.

FOUR
Triggering an Ice Age

Now the occurrence of global warming actually triggers an ice age. That is, we are seeing the same principle in operation, regarding climate changes, as observed in the description of the operation of a refrigerator's regulation of temperature in Chapter Two. This is where the theory outlined in this work differs from some alternative schemes, as revealed in Chapter Three, because the actions of these other schemes are randomised. As has been outlined previously, 'Sod's Law' ensures what can happen, will happen: Earth would have experienced a run-away temperature in one direction or the other before now and neither the reader nor the author would be alive to debate this issue.

So, we have a circulating Gulf Stream and global warming underlay: a set of events shown to be occurring because the polar ice-caps are receding towards their respective poles. Now, ice formations discard many of the 'additives' that water suspends whilst in its liquid state, and one of these rejected materials is salt. (Many readers will be aware that common ice cubes from a fridge can be used as an alternative to distilled water when we top up our maintainable car batteries). So the ice caps are melting due to the fact that raised temperatures or global warming is occurring and as a result, diluting the salty sea water. Since salty water is denser than fresh water, i.e. is heavier per unit volume, the diluted or salt-free water becomes less heavy than its salty 'cousin', and the less salty water is unable to sink as readily. As a consequence, the Golf Stream flow slows. In fact this 'slowing' of the Gulf Stream flow has already been recently reported by oceanographers along with the supporting information that digging into the ocean bed directly below the aforementioned 'stream' reveals successive layers of large and small shells left behind by deceased molluscs.

The interpretation these specialist scientists attached to the above findings is that the food supply available to these dead shellfish relics varied in quantity according to the climate and mode the 'Stream' experienced at the time. The reported finding appears to support this work's earlier assertion that climate change is a cyclic occurrence and, any time soon, in geological terms, the flow will come to a grinding halt. Herein, ladies and gentlemen, are the required conditions that facilitate an ice age!

Clearly, with the event of an ice age the ice-caps will re-generate and the sea will slowly return to its previous salty condition and thereby reach a state which will permit the Gulf Stream to recommence its heat distributing flow. But this type of event is massive in nature and it will take a long time to re-establish 'normality'. In the meantime food will become unobtainable. The stocks of this essential commodity will promptly run down even providing transport links are maintained. Recalling the state of UK public transport systems when just a few leaves or flakes of snow fall, it is unlikely that the system of public transport will function for more than a few days into the forecast ice age! As Sir Fred Hoyle relates in his book 'ICE' (published by Hutchinson in 1981) we will only be able to survive in tiny groups, similar to the Eskimo lifestyle, because fish will survive beneath ice several feet thick. Our political 'Masters,'under the auspices of the late PM E. Heath, have again 'messed matters up' by giving UK fish to Europe and have realised of late that the fish stocks of GB's coastal waters are immature and down to crisis level now - one really couldn't make the story up. How our politicians look us in the eye while talking of honesty and trust, convincing us they are worthy of ever increasing salaries, is nothing short of incomprehensible.

It is evident that the period between the events described in Chapters Two and Three may be variable but it's clear that the event of global warming triggers an ice age and the event of an ice age triggers a return to a warm age. The duration of an ice age means that it will be difficult, to say the least, for all life-forms to be sustained and survive. Many life-forms will perish to the point of extinction and some species will inevitably be lost but a few hardy, well prepared humans will survive and life will continue to exist, eventually reverting to what we now consider 'normality' on planet Earth.

After an indeterminate number of ice ages and global warming periods, an unrelated 'Big Bang' will occur and in the event of such an occurrence there will be no local survivors. However, before we consider such an outlook, we first need to understand more about the 'Big Bang Theory' and this is the focus of the next chapter.

FIVE

The cause of 'The Big Bang'

The 'Big Bang' is thought to be a random occurrence which occurs when certain criteria are met in a 'ripening' black hole. Effectively, a black hole consists of a gravity hot-spot which attracts matter to itself. It is suspected, depending on the amount and type of matter available to be sucked into a black hole, that the finished product may turn out to be a Sun star or the birth of a new galaxy.

The difficulty of investigating a black hole is that the gravitational force exerted is so great that anything that gets sucked in to its 'internals' is crunched up to a miniature sized ingot* for the want of a better word. It is said, incorrectly I believe, that nothing escapes a black hole's clutches , not even light. Accordingly, optical and instrumental investigations are difficult or even non starters. One, it is said, can only observe the way its gravitational influence affects surrounding matter. As a related point of consideration, the author was fortunate enough to obtain a series of photographs of our Galaxy the Milky Way. The images were taken by the Hubble telescope's camera from its orbital positions around our planet. It shows a flat spiral of matter and gas culminating with a black spot at the centre or hub of this enormous galaxy - much like a Catherine wheel firework. Personal speculation gives rise to the prospect that the centre point maybe a black hole - one which is perhaps contemplating enjoying 'our' galaxy as 'lunch'!

* An ingot is a material that is cast into a shape suitable for further processing.

Formulating a theory which clearly describes the 'Big Bang' has occupied the author's thoughts for some 50 years or more. But the information that finally seemed to produce an understanding of this occurrence was obtained in the 1970s, but the connection between that information and the 'Big Bang' did not actually occur until the summer of 2007. (A delay of this magnitude may give some indication of the limitations of mankind's reasoning abilities) However, it would be helpful to have a miniature working model of a black hole and separately the 'Big Bang' to test theories and begin to understand future ramifications for planet Earth and its inhabitants. Fortunately, the author has been able to devise or describe models that produce occurrences which seem to approximate to the behaviour of both phenomena.

In the latter part of the autumn of 2007 it was realised that an engine based on the principles of the 'Big Bang' might be possible to achieve. It was considered that, with proper development, the engine might be a useful tool to assist in navigating the Earth to a new spot in space, which might enable the globe to orbit another Sun star. But these speculations, which will be considered here, are for the distant but foreseeable future when, for example, our present Sun has exhausted its supply of usable hydrogen.

To improve the Reader's ability to follow the train of thought outlined in this work – relating to what is thought to occur in a black hole prior to a 'Big Bang' and during a 'Big Bang', the sequence of events leading to this explanation is given in the following text.

A black hole is, as previously stated, a gravity hotspot which forces or attracts all nearby matter into its core. It is thought that these items are often, if not always, surrounded by a spiral of gas or other space debris, probably because of the enormous gravitational pull exerted by the said hotspot. It occurred to the author that a whirlpool system seemed to approximately reflect the formation of a black hole. As a result, the kitchen sink was commandeered to explore a makeshift test-bed. Providing the drain is centrally positioned and its diameter is large enough and clear of debris, then a whirlpool will develop from the draining water without assistance from the observer. It is representative of a galaxy because it has a 'gravity hotspot' and 'space debris' in the form of water, soapsuds or food particles. The use or formation of a whirlpool is the fastest and most efficient way of getting rid of washing up water as can be verified by timing the event and comparing the result with time taken to drain a similar amount of debris when the whirlpool is not invoked. It is a fact that nature always seems to develop or utilise the most efficient way of achieving its own ends.

Furthermore, observations and manipulations reveal that the speed of rotation of a kitchen-sink whirlpool, once formed, can be easily slowed or even stopped by introducing a small flow of water from a partially turned on tap into its flank. We will return to the possible use of this observation in due course, but for now this experiment seems to show the generalised workings of the Milky Way galaxy and its probable black hole centre point.

During the '70s, the author worked in the Physics department of a research company and became interested in the technique of plating or coating plastic material with metal coatings. One will probably have experienced the frustrating business of trying to repair a broken plastic device by gluing the material to the detached piece. Admittedly, there are specialist glues such as plumbers use to join PVC plastic pipes or the use of ether to temporarily dissolve and subsequently stick perspex sections together, but that aside, the process of gluing plastic usually presents a dubious or hopeless situation. How then, I wondered, did manufactures of plastic items manage to attach a thin skin of metal to a plastic object?

One day, having engaged the Head of Department with this query, he reliably informed me that the plastic object that required plating was placed in a vacuum chamber. A pair of terminals which are connected via an external switch to a suitable electric supply are attached or clamped to a bar of metal – chromium, for example. The vessel is then sealed and its internal pressure reduced. When a satisfactory degree of vacuum is reached the external switch is put to the 'on' position. The chromium is then heated to its vaporising temperature and the resultant material explodes 'sphere wise', obviously trying to fill the vacuum it now 'inhabits'. In so doing it coats the plastic object. The 'adhesion result' of this coating procedure is molecular and almost permanent.

You might say: how did this particular industrial technique reveal the nature and origins of a 'Big Bang'? Well, the two events are not absolutely identical but are similar in nature. We have said earlier that the black hole takes in enormous amounts of space debris and crunches the material 'sucked in' into a very tiny ingot. The jargon usually utilised to describe this process is 'enormous amounts of matter is taken and squeezed into a matchbox-sized ingot under the extreme force of gravity that exists in the centre of a black hole'.

It therefore stands to reason that there is extreme pressure in the centre of a black hole. Now, as we have already stated, pressure generates heat and extreme pressure generates extreme temperatures. At some point the black hole will 'ripen' by generating sufficient heat to vaporize the content of its core. At that point the resultant pressure will become non-containable and the extremely high pressured gases will endeavour to spread out and fill the vacuum it finds itself inhabiting, with what can only be described as unimaginable force. And there you have the event of a big bang!' Because the random content of debris that caused this explosion is almost bound to contain some radioactive material, the presence of that radioactivity in the aftermath will probably be associated with a nuclear explosion. In the author's view, however, this is probably not the case. But it may well be that the initial explosion just described can, under some conditions, produce sufficient pressure to the already heated interior of the black hole that may cause a secondary role involving a nuclear event.

There are two types of nuclear heat producing processes - these are termed 'Fission' and 'Fusion'. Fission describes a method of producing heat that is employed in current nuclear-driven electric generating stations. The heat producing part of the system utilises uranium fuel rods held in close proximity to one another and generated heat is utilised to produce steam, which drives a conventional turbine and alternator. Control of the heat generated is obtained by altering the space between the fuel rods or by introducing a 'calming' shield between the fuel rods. A suitable material for this function is carbon or graphite and if these materials break up or the 'calming' mechanism fails, then the system can go into meltdown and an explosion results - as occurred in Chernobyl during the last century.

Fusion is name of the type of nuclear heat producing technique that is utilised by our Sun star. To initiate this type of procedure, exceedingly high temperatures and pressures are needed. And it may be that the 'Big Bang' explosion described in the preceding paragraph provides the necessary 'start up process' of a Fusion system or, if the materials undergoing this treatment are suitable, an unlikely situation for the most part, a so-called hydrogen bomb explosion may occur.

I can hear the reader thinking: but how do we know if the foregoing is an accurate account of the facts? Well, one can't be completely sure that the author's account is 100% accurate, since no one really knows what happens inside a black hole - a device/process which endeavours to keep its secrets to itself.

Mathematicians will give a suggested theory consideration, no doubt. Now, from the author's perspective, mathematics is like poetry in motion, offering solutions to complex problems provided, of course, the mathematical model being used to solve the issue at hand is accurate - but this idealised viewpoint only holds if one is able to insert the correct data into the equations being manipulated. And how can one do that if one cannot gain access to the 'goings on' inside a black hole? All we can conclude is that the explanation given in the foregoing text regarding the causes and aftermath of the 'Big Bang' is practical (as shown by the plastic plating process described previously), comprehensible and plausible. Furthermore, the suggestion given within this book that climate change is cyclic and a 'Big Bang' occurs when a black hole is ripe is also based on logic. So, if the given mechanism thought responsible for these phenomena is subsequently challenged by equally convincing theories, this new information will not necessarily alter the need for suggested avoidance schemes promoted herein.

To continue, it is possible to demonstrate or relate the erroneous results that mathematics and mathematicians can produce by referring to Marconi's experiment that took place at the beginning of the last century. Marconi announced his intention of transmitting a signal from Land's End in Cornwall to Newfoundland in Canada - a matter of some 3000 miles separated the two points. The mathematicians of the day rightly told the experimenter that since radio signals of the day could not penetrate the ocean or the crust of our Planet and that the experiment would fail. Fortunately, the experimenter went ahead with his experiment and succeeded in his mission, whereupon the mathematicians informed the radio enthusiast how his experiment succeeded! The signal had in fact bounced off one of the 'layers' that encircle our globe, way, way, above our heads. Incidentally, the technique accidentally employed in this work was the forerunner of a modern equivalent, i.e. communication satellites: a system that is more reliable than ionosphere utilisation, even though the Military used the ionosphere for the purpose of distant radio communication well into 1970s. The event of the Russian Sputnik, the world's first man made orbiting satellite did not occur until the October of 1957, an event which was reported as the author returned to the UK on the Cunard's 'Corinthia' in preparation for departure to the frozen Canadian North land.

And then there is hypocrisy, a trait that sometimes rears its ugly head in matters of progress or attempted progress. I quote Harrison's experience with his chronometer. In the eighteenth century the nautical navigational technique was lacking a vital ability. That is, it was not possible to calculate or establish longitude at sea because accurate time keeping was not possible afloat. The globe had been divided, in an east/west manner, into twenty-four 'pole to pole' divisions, which correspond to 15 degree or 1 hour segments. Thus, being able to transfer a time zone (Greenwich Time was chosen as reference) to a local position with accuracy would enable a mariner to compare local and Greenwich time differences.

Converting the time difference to degrees enabled a longitudinal position to be obtained by the simple method of converting time differences to degrees of longitude east or west of Greenwich. (Latitudinal information can, and could, of course, be obtained by measuring the angle between the horizontal and the polar star, sometimes termed the North star or Polaris) But such ability for calculating longitude demanded accurate time keeping at sea, so the British Government offered £10,000 reward for the first man to produce a clock capable of keeping time to the accuracy of one second per month at sea. Harrison succeeded in achieving this aim, but the horologists of the day blocked Harrison's claim to the prize money on the grounds he wasn't a qualified horologist! For completeness sake, Harrison achieved his aim to keep time at sea by employing an extra large balance wheel which, being heavy, exhibited inertia, thereby resisting the otherwise upset that would be caused to his gimballed* clock by a rolling ship. His third and successful time-piece is still maintained in running order to this very day at Greenwich Observatory SW London.

* A device for suspending something so that it will remain substantially level when the support is tipped.

A similar example can be shown for Galileo, who invented the telescope. His seventeenth century observations concluded, correctly, that Earth is a minor planet orbiting the Sun. However, this reasoning clashed with the beliefs of the Vatican at the time who promptly directed the scholar to recant or be imprisoned. However, this author appreciates the difference twixt valid criticism and hypocrisy, and accepts the necessity for (and potential benefit of) valid criticism.

Additions to Chapter 5 Issue 3

The foregoing, contained in Chapter 5, explains what is believed to be an accurate description of the demise of a 'Black Hole' since there are events which indicate, or seem to indicate, what is happening at the time of consideration. So it maybe time to consider the start of a 'Black Hole', within the limits of Human knowledge, of how a Black Hole is started and a Galaxy is formed.

Investigation of the known sources of matter exhibiting the principles of attraction of matter do not appear adequate, that is that their attraction or gravitational force is too weak to provide a system known as a 'Black Hole'. But the existance of 'Dark Matter' which provides the opposite effect of a 'Gravitation Field' was considered a possible answer even though the amount of force exhibited by such an assembly is not known. But it is impossible to form the Dark Matter whereby it could produce a Black Hole. But it is thought, & according to Hoyle, that the Universe is expanding, in all probability, partially due to the influence of this secretive force.

So the obvious solution to this problem of Black Hole formation seems to require the existance of a new material which would have to provide a considerable increase in 'gravitational pull' when compared with 'normal'space matter.....a substance we will call 'Super Gravatational Field' or an 'SGF'.

So assuming such a matter exists, & it seems that it must exist, it would have to exhibit an extremely powerful attracting ability. It may even be that an 'SGF' force is an essential force to form a Galaxy, & since the contents of Space is said to be expanding, one can easily see that matter attracted to an 'SGF' would have to be deflected by the additional force of, perhaps, Dark Matter....hence forming the closing spiral condition that surrounds a 'Black Hole'..

And that seems to be about as far as one can go at this time in explaining about the origins of a Black Hole & Galaxy. But the writer has little doubt that a method of investigating and confirming this suspected condition will be found in the future. Especially since 'our' ultimate survival depends upon knowing fully about the the physical effects that surround us.

Additions to Chapter 5- Issue 4

A further possibility for evading the destruction of Planet Earth BEFORE the core of our Galaxy reaches the point of exploding is given which maybe easier to put into place & carries less risk of the destruction of Planet Earth. As reported earlier, the Solar System consists of the Sun & a number of Planets which are held together by the Sun's Gravitational Force. The Sun is held in our Galaxy by the Milky Way's central Gravity Force. If this Black Hole was 'destroyed' before it had 'ripened' [a matter which is thought to be imminent], the Solar System would be free to travel in space. Further, if this freedom was given to the Solar System when it would be forced to travel toward a chosen Galaxy with an aim of 'being captured'....it would give the controller the ability to repeat the seeking of another Galaxy if the first choice was not suitable by a repeat of the outlined procedure given above. This outlined procedure is thought to provide less risk to Planet Earth than the methods previously described. The prospect of deciding if a Black Hole was approaching its explosive condition could be achieved by measuring the temperature of its core [see detail in earlier part of this chapter] ...if the knowledge to enable such a test was available at this time. But the Galaxy has been 'filling' with matter for a long, long time & is probably about due to errupt. This problem maybe delayed by injecting a coolant into the core of the Milky Way & then endevouring to decimate the Black Hole with a number of Hydrogen Bombs. Loss of Solar Planets other than the Earth or the Sun through collision whilst in transit are not thought to affect the re-positioning of Planet Earth. This procedure may sound a bit drastic but faiure to act on it will result in...........
April 2016

Additions to Chapter 5 - Issue 5

'It was considered necessary to add to the content of Issue 4 which was written in April 2016. with Issue 5, which was written in June 2017.

Replacing the position of the Solar System to our nearest Galaxy might impose some problems.

The first point is that the distance to our nearest Galaxy is only expressed as an approximation because of difficulties in getting a clear image of this distant object due to matter interposed between the Galaxies. Without the true distance between the Galaxies & the velocity achieved by a 'released' Solar System' one cannot determine the transit time of such a journey... Nor can one determine.if there is a 'spare sun' available for use to complement the needs of Earth with a supply of heat to compensate for 'our probably almost burnt out sun '. But even if our sun fails to last the transit time of the proposed journey, it is thought, an increase in life support facilities will have been achieved on Earth.because, as previously stated, the Milky Way Core is probably about due to errupt - finalising all Earth Bound Life.

Additionally it would be possible to release the Solar System so that it just travelled in space without a goal or that it persued a path that is employed by Comets. Admittedly, there is a problem that the Solar System travelling in fresh space may meet problems with obstructions such as radiation, a planet or other blockages. But this problem also exists with the current journey of the our Planet Earth which encircles the sun. And the sun drags our planet Earth round the core of our Galaxy.....without RECENT mishap,. In fact altering our space position may even avoid a potential mishap!'

It was earlier suggested, in Edition 4, that by successfully attacking the core of our Galaxy with H Bombs that the Solar System would be free to travel in space & could be directed to take up a given course by the point of orbit around the Black Hole that the Solar System was 'released'. And this is a satisfactory statement if the exact time of the Black Hole erruption was possible to establish. All that can be said is such disruption is 'about to happen' due to the excessive amount of time the Black Hole has been collecting space material & the progress of its internal temperature rise....since these non-measurable factors cause Black Holes to errupt. Apart from the uncertain data, it is thought that method of causing an escape route for the Solar System was efficient & a fairly risk free option. However, there is a further possible snag which needs to be addressed. In view of the fact that the exact timing of the Central Black Hole Explosion cannot be established & its huge distance from Earth, a revised escape procedure for removing the Solar System out of its present Milky Way 'Home' needs to be considered. Due to the inability to give certainty to these events ....i e, the given suggestion maybe unuseable without a 'risk' of failure. Hence the certainty of the scheme is not definite because the EXACT remaining 'length of life' of the core of our Galaxy is not PRECISELY known..

We therefore need to consider alternative release methods for the Solar System. The explosion of a series of Hydrogen Bombs correctly positioned from the sun would cancel the effect of gravity from the Milky Way Black Hole & free the Solar System. But this approach would demand sufficent force to be generated to cancel the force that holds the Solar System in place if the process was not to fail. It maybe that a series of spaced explosions would be more likely to be successful. It is concluded the adoption of this scheme MAY be more certain of success than the method outlined in Edition 4...a scheme which was partially duplicated in the proceding paragraph.

Of course, some will consider the schemes outlined to be too risky....but to do nothing would open us up to destruction of all Earthbound Life in an estimated 'short time' period! A short time period because the event of failure would not depend on the length of life left in the sun as indicated in some quarters ....but would depend on the Milky Way Black Hole remainimg in a stable condition.

Considering the overall content of this Book, it would appear advisable to decrease the size & powers of a number of Government Establishments & the extent of World Wide population levels in order to free un-necessary expense & other complications, such as the Work in this Book describes, that appears to be threatening the continuity of Earth Bound Life.

Additions to Chapter 5 – Issue 6

It was evident in 2017 that further information regarding the removal of the Solar System from its position in the MILKY WAY GALAXY maybe a helpful lead to the escape of this SOLAR SYSTEM from our Galaxy. Hence this final addition dated 1st June, 2018.

This step would be assisted by placing an imaginary Cone between the circumference of The Sun and the Black Hole that forms the centre of our Galaxy, The Milky Way. The diameter of the Cones Base should equal the diameter of the Sun and the tip of the Cone should reach the circumference of our central Black Hole. The release of the Solar System from its 'home' in our Galaxy would require the cancellation of the gravitational force from the core of our Galaxy which travels via the position of our 'Cone'. And since the Sun orbits the Black Hole that centres our Galaxy, the Cone would obviously need repositioning to continue showing the needed removal of the holding gravitational force on the Solar System.

Exploring the effect of H Bomb explosions at either extremity of the 'Cone' would show that a single explosion at the Black Hole end of our Cone would cancel the hold on the Solar System.....but the distance from Earth to the edge of the Milky Way Black Hole is approximately 27 K Light Years distant! Looking at the Sun end of the Cone, the Distance from Earth is a mere 91 Million Miles. However, the number of H Bombs needed to free the Solar System from the effects of the Milky Way gravitational force would multiply from one Bomb to an unrealistic number of Bombs per shot. Therefore an intermediate position would have to be adopted for 'repelling' the Gravitational Force that holds the Solar System 'in place.

Unfortunately, the available choice of activating Rockets to achieve a suitable attack on the Gravitational Force put out by The Milky Way in the suggested third position of attack on the Gravitational Force holding the Solar System in place is unknown to the Writer. The necessary choice must be available but would probably be a military secret. It is known that Russian President Putin has announced that his Country has developed a Super High Speed Rocket but its range or performance is unknown to the Writer. However, the development of a purpose built Rocket should not be too expensive to design if needed.....since the device is required to protect the lives of all Earth Bound Species.

Additions to Chapter 5 – Issue 7

An article in The Daily Mail, dated October 27/ 2018, page 57 shows a Rocket which can be launched from a modified 747 at around 35,000 feet & can put moderate loads into Orbit. It looks as though its a method that might be successful in placing a Hydrogen Bomb in the correct position to repel the gravitation force generated by The Milky Way Galaxy that holds the Solar System in its place. The system is produced by Vergin Orbit.needs investigating to find out if it would do the job of separating the Solar System from the Milky Way.Galaxy as described earlier in Chapter 5.'

Additions to Chapter 5 – Issue 8

The mentally derived theory regarding Black Hole's final behaviour contained in Edition 1 of this publication was written up in 2007/8 & published in 2011 in the USA. This information was also contained in Edition 2,3,4,5,6, & 7 & published in the UK.

But Doctor Glacintucci, who resides in Australia, has written up the detection of a Black Hole Explosion which occurred millions of years ago thus finally backing up my claims & which finally dismisses the Physicists recently dismissed claim that Black Holes do not explode. A brief report of this information appears in the Daily Mail dated 29th February 2020 page 3.

SIX

Navigating our Globe through Space

With regard to changing our globe's position in space to avoid, for example, the terminal and freezing condition that the demise of our sun will cause, it may be prudent to consider avoidance. One such alternative regarding re-siting the Earth's position in space in order to take advantage of another, younger, or man produced Sun star is suggested in the following section. The scheme, if successful, would offer the prospect of allowing Earth to continue providing a 'good home' to humanity and all other species that share this planet with us. It also provides an alternative aim - that we 'seed' another suitable planet with limited numbers of selected persons that can be crammed into a space ship. (First suggested by the author in 1992: See Ref 4 Attached.) This idea of repositioning our sphere may conjure up all sorts of objections, such as the upheaval a scheme of this nature would incur. But we are talking survival here and the choice is stark. Endeavour and succeed, or perish!

The idea of global relocation stems from the theory put forward to describe the 'Big Bang'. The theory suggested a form of space engine to the author based on the principle of the 'Big Bang'. A suggestion that such a scheme might be possible is mentioned at the beginning of Chapter Five. Claims of this nature are speculative, but they are founded on observed results of experiment and therefore merit the need for further investigation or development. And who will be bold enough to deny the possibility of such projected ideas?

My grandfather had a son, my father, born at the turn of the twentieth century and if someone had approached my granddad at that time and informed him that his son would live through the era of the successful demonstration of the first heavier-than-air flying machine, wireless communication, telephone conversations, television, radar, penicillin and humans walking on the lunar surface, he would have given the informer more than a wry look and would probably have directed him to the nearest lunatic asylum. With the aid of hindsight the old chap would have been out of order. So, let us not be too quick to condemn the prospect of such a scheme suggested in the above and following text.

In order to appreciate the proposal to move our sphere to orbit a younger Sun star we need to ask the question: what holds the Earth in its present position in space? The answer is pretty obviously the gravitational pull of our Sun star modified by the centrifugal force generated by our globe's orbital function around the sun. In fact the sun holds the whole solar system in place as well. The next query to be investigated is: what holds our sun in its present position? The answer to that question is thought to be the gravitational hot-spot situated in the centre of the Milky Way galaxy. The position that our Sun star holds relative to the centre of the Milky Way galaxy will be modified by the centrifugal force generated by the Solar System's spiral path being traced out as it 'screws' its way toward the centre of our galaxy. Whether or not individual galaxies are held together in a similar fashion to the description just given with respect to the Solar System and its relationship with the Milky Way is open to debate. This is because some astronomers believe the Universe is still expanding from the effects of the last 'Big Bang'. This belief opens up the possibility that the galaxies are not bound together by the use of gravitational and orbital effects described for the Solar System; but are in effect in 'free fall'.

We must also mention the possibility that dark matter is responsible for the reported expansion of the universe since this illusive substance exhibits the reverse characteristics to ordinary or negatively charged matter with which we are familiar.* But mankind's knowledge of the 'total Universe' is too limited to enable facts or firm descriptions to be given. Of course, one could project the idea that it is impossible to steer a straight course in space whether we are talking about a catapulted stone, a NASA space rocket (or according to A.E.) a beam of light**, because gravity intervenes and a curved path is followed by the 'projectiles or emissions'.

**It is a fact that has since shown by observation that light is deflected by gravitational influence.

If we now return to the observation reported in Chapter Five, we will recall the promise of a return to the point raised about a tiny jet of water injected into the flank of a spiral of water, soapsuds and food particles that modifies or even stops the kitchen sink whirlpool dead in its tracks. So, since it seems as though a kitchen sink whirlpool is a comparatively easy affair to manipulate, there would appear to be no reason to suppose that a space- based spiral would be different in principle although the difference in scale obviously will require much more force to achieve a similar effect.

It follows then that if we humans developed the afore-mentioned space engine, it maybe possible with the aid of a few, some or many atomic devices placed and detonated in strategic positions of the Milky Way spiral to modify the Solar System's positional holding force, and thereby change our globe's position in space. Embarking on a venture as described in the previous sentence would obviously need some preparation such as a store of food, shelter from the expected lowered temperatures that would be experienced from such a voyage. There would also be the need for a 'bed' to take care of expected gravitational and other changes in forces that would probably be experienced, as well as a need for the zoos of this globe to provide a 'Noah's Arc' to aid in the survival of the planet's wildlife, perhaps in the form of sperm, eggs & seeds. The suggested global repositioning scheme may also enable approximate continuity of life as we currently know it.

There may even be the need or possibility of a practice run depending on our Sun star's demise characteristics. For example, if the sun gradually reduces its heat output it may become advantageous to shift our orbit a little closer to it in its dying 'moments' and that would give the opportunity for a mini practice 'trip' in space. It should be clearly understood that the foregoing information is NOT a properly calculated space venture. It merely raises the prospect of the possibility of escaping a freezing demise when the Sun star uses up its supply of hydrogen, for example.

In actuality, if one succeeded in completely stopping the Milky Way spiral of space matter, the entire Solar System might find itself at the centre of our galaxy ahead of the present timetable. However, I am confident that some bright young astrophysicist will be able to work out the fine detail of what it is that needs to be done to modify the Milky Way spiral and effectively steer our globe to a 'sunnier spot' elsewhere in space when the time is right to do so. It would be prudent to remind the reader that if the above proposal were to be carried out, the upset caused to other planetary system's orbital paths might cause offence if these globes are inhabited by intelligent life! It may be that such actions and results would initiate inter-planetary warfare!

*NB The prospect exists that the use of 'dark matter' may assist in the development of a everyday 'anti-gravity mat'. As mentioned elsewhere, a specialised 'anti gravity mat', utilising centrifugal force, and capable of limited deployment can be shown to exist....and is currently better known as an International Space Station!

SEVEN
Population Growth and Levels

Population growth appears to be officially approved by most Governments, a deduction arrived at since there is little or no voiced disapproval of the theme. Quite the reverse in fact! The exception is China and they have obviously found coping with a population level of some one billion souls or more too much of a strain generally. India has a similar number of souls to provide for and, although one politician attempted to control that climbing population level she, Mrs Ghandi, abandoned the scheme in the face of public protest.

The problem is that when we consider a climbing worldwide population level of some seven billion people, ongoing food supply is tenuous. India and China have rubbed along on a pretty low standard of living up until the present time. But both countries are now emerging economic miracles and are upsetting the commodity markets with their increased demands for raw materials. As their economic strength grows they will, rightly, demand, pay for, and obtain an increased share of the world's already strained food supply. But someone may say that our UK supermarkets are awash with food, a true fact of life, and therefore assume there is nothing to be concerned about. But it isn't like that worldwide, and many, especially in Africa, are suffering from starvation. This is partly due to unscrupulous politicians and would-be leaders squabbling at the expense of the unfortunate African people. Added to this problem is that there are too many people living off the resources available, and that applies to water especially. Assistance is often given by charitable organisations based elsewhere, but in general terms they are not thought to be helping the situation. When food 'handouts' temporarily end famine the people do what all of nature's species do. They retire to the bush for a time and re-emerge later with new members of their family. A similar reasoning can be extended to the unfortunate Pakistani people who suffer from repeated flooding disasters, i.e. too many people.....living on a flood plain! These 'rescue' situations can only prevail in the short term.

This urge to renew ourselves and expand the numbers of our kind has been given unwise political impetuses by the agreement reached at the Rio Environmental Summit in the 1990's when the Nations of the World met to hammer out their environmental policies. Professor Doll is believed to have been reported as recommending that the world wide human population could safely be increased from the then current five billion to something like three billion extra souls, providing enough trees (it is believed the words 'many millions' were recommended) were planted to sop up the extra CO_2 that would thereby be produced. The author did not and does not agree with this adopted opinion. Excessive tree planting density, high-density population levels and necessary food production requirements do not go smoothly hand in hand! Our forefathers knew this because, unlike to days 'food experts' they lived close to Mother Nature.

The problem partially lies with nature's programming of all its species. Take yeast, for example. This micro-organism occurs on the skin of grapes growing in the vineyard. It is used to ferment beer, wine and in the production of some breads. Its part in said production of drinks is to produce the alcohol content of these refreshments. And provided the temperature and pH values are satisfactory, it will consume any sugar present in the fluid, until it pollutes its environment with the rising alcohol level or eats itself out of food, i.e. sugar. The same or similar process exists in a gardener's compost heap. The micro-organisms simply eat their way through the waste vegetable matter until there is no more food left for them to eat and, as a result, most of the little creatures perish from starvation.

If one takes note of the numbers of huge lorries that convey food stocks to UK Supermarkets all day and all night long, then one may begin to wonder where it comes from. And if one ever tried growing food, the experience might make the reader wonder even more so, particularly if the grower was unfortunate enough to encounter adverse conditions of the type imposed on the author in the '60s and 70s! The fact remains that human beings outdo even locusts when it comes to devouring food crops!

It would be neglectful not to mention Genetically Modified (GM) food. The would-be blessings are undoubted, but one has to balance these against the risks that GM foods present when they have not been thoroughly tested, in spite of what the experts believe or tell us they believe. I will never forget the picture of Right Hon Gummer who was, I believe, Food & Agriculture Secretary at the time, sharing a beef-burger with his daughter to show how safe the tasty morsel was! The gentleman was undoubtedly assured by EXPERTS that beef-burgers were safe, but at the time, i.e. 1990, few knew about the protein 'Prion' which was lurking in beef that was improperly fed. The protein caused Creutzfeldt-Jakob Disease in humans.. This exposure, which fortunately doesn't seem to have caused either the Right Hon Gentleman or his daughter a problem so far, only shows that improperly tested GM foods may contain dangerous substances that nobody knows anything about until...

Our political 'masters', including Ex Prime Minister, Tony Blair, do not seem to realise the harm they have done to our nation by the wholesale surrendering of GB's sovereignty to the EU. For example, a report dated September 3, 2003: 'Britain is told by EU you cannot ban GM crops!

This statement is followed up by the Daily Mail's leader 'Frankenfoods: the damning proof' which seemingly exposes the plight experienced by Canadian farmers who undertook a full blown trial of growing GM oilseed rape. Not only were the yields reported as down on conventional crops but the weeds were said to be 'infected' by the GM crops altered genes and over a period became dominant in their growth pattern, and were generally out of control.

So the picture regarding food supplies looks far from rosy without considering the matter of the impending ice age. Impending, that is, if one accepts the reasoning revealed in Chapter Four. What will happen then is we will have famine, Arctic conditions and 90% or more of the population of Europe will come to a horrible and miserable end. But our global politicians are too busy trying to stop global warming occurring to consider the given warning or to seek workable solutions to the problem.

But halting global warming is an impossible and perhaps even a dangerous task! The few humans who do survive will be those who can catch or obtain fish, a life form that which will survive the icy conditions. But the fish stocks in the English Channel have been made available to our European Cousins and consequently fish stocks there (and elsewhere) are at an all time low. So the 'ice age outlook' is bleak: with zero fruit, vegetables, meat or adequate fish production. In the circumstances, it would seem to the author that surrendered UK Border and Immigration Controls need to be regained and placed firmly under the control of dedicated UK politicians. And a word about Fertility Clinics. The National Budget allotted to this facility is not known but it is thought to be sizeable. And if this is the case, it is one more policy that seems to be at odds with the theme this work is trying to promote...that is the application of common sense in place of political expedience or dogma.

The author thinks it goes without saying that, a 'big thank you' is not due to our seemingly nonlistening, unaffordable, unfit-for-purpose political 'masters' and their plans for globalisation. Nor must we forget their apparent lack of foresight or their stubborn inability to 'back track'! * And this paragraph omits to mention that we, the UK Public, have never been consulted about joining the EU Community in spite of the promise of a referendum on the matter. In passing, it is thought that the Political Set will not appreciate the revelations and opinions given in this work. But they have, between them, ignored repeated warnings in letter and report form and it seems many of their Constituents do not appreciate what is being implemented in their names! . So what else can one do to obtain attention to matters that obviously need consideration to say the very least?

* The newly formed Coalition Government headed by PM David Cameron seems to show some signs of willlingness to reform but it is too early to make a serious appraisal of this administration's efforts to curb excesses and waste.

EIGHT
Introduction to Political Shortcomings

Political shortcomings appear to have been in evidence throughout most of this book, assuming one accepts the information, logic and theories put forward. It is now time to be more precise in the revelations that lead to the claim of 'POLITICAL SHORTCOMINGS'.

High on the list of 'shortcomings' is the politician's attitude and legislation towards trees because these matters affect people's main assets and rights in life i.e. a reasonable degree of safety for property and person, plus safe food production or even food production full-stop!

We have had a glimpse of the effect that overcrowded trees can have on food production in Chapter One. In case there are readers who shrug their shoulders and say the author has admitted that he knew little of the requirements of growing food at that time, be assured that there is other proof of misuse or abuse lurking 'in the wings'. For example, England was graced with a goodly supply of beautiful elm trees until the '70s strike of so called Dutch Elm Disease. And the results of this affliction, which occurs and spreads, by cooperation between insects and fungus WAS THE UK's LOSS OF THE ELM TREE SPECIE. Even so, it must be pointed out here that an equally devastating occurrence can be obtained by fungus or insects working in isolation! And the author experienced the proof of all these statements many times during the period of vandalism inflicted by misuse of power granted to LAs in the form of TPOs. Silver Leaf and Armillaria (also known as American Boot Lace Disease) for example, can kill almost any tree, although the Plum Tree remains the main target of Silver Leaf.

Furthermore, the author, during the 1970's, became involved with a frost protection problem of a fruit grower in Hertfordshire who planted an orchard on dwarf root stocks at a density of about 1800 trees per acre (the tree spacing was 4 feet x 6 feet.) The gentleman, who made a success of this densely planted orchard, used to prune these miniature trees on a year round basis to prevent inter twining of branches and foliage. Failure to do so would have produced a sheltered environment, which would have encouraged the infestation of insects, and these infestations would have decimated his pear and apple crop. This pruning exercise had to be backed by routine spraying which meant the spray apparatus was almost in daily use throughout the growing season. Although the orchard was a success, he privately informed me he would not repeat that density of planting in any future endeavours.

As already stated, the control of these pests, fungi and diseases they cause to food crops, soil and other plant life is almost impossible when these afflictions occur in epidemic form due to 'suitable' condition or environment caused by over-crowded tree populations. Attempts to do so in the USA during the 70's caused human birth deformities through the use of powerful anti-fungal sprays and insecticides. And the excessive use of these chemicals can also set up cancer in adult humans if the substances become too heavily involved with the food chain or the air we breathe!

The author can recall examples of overcrowded forestation in the province of Quebec, where pine trees were being grown with little or no spacing between individual plantings. The air was liberally populated with little black beetle-type insects that gave a painful nip when given the opportunity to settle on one's person. And the horizon was filled with columns of thick smoke issuing from closely spaced apparatuses - smoke to which the author has ascribed the term 'insecticide emissions'.

People who seem to worship trees in highly dense planting densities rarely seem to care or even be aware of the problems their dreams cause when these aspirations become realities by being put into practice. What appears to be missing in these tree-worshippers' minds is the fact that one cannot make good an excess in one sphere, say excess human population levels, by creating an excess in another sphere, say excessive and over-crowded afforestation. You have to, regardless of fad or phobia, moderate both activities to provide a balanced environment, which means a drastic reduction of global human population levels too!

Then there is the public endorsement, by prominent politicians of GB, of privately and publicly funded forestry organisations in England. The people who control some of these organisations were, and in all probability still are, creating new forests by planting out oaks at about a two-metre spacing. We will 'dissect' the detail of one of these examples so that all can appreciate what is really being said here.

There is, and the author quotes from it, a page from a magazine dated June 2005, (See Ref 1 attached), which shows Andrew Beer standing in front of a semi-mature tree of unknown species.

The gentleman is reported as being a member of the Woodland Trust and is in charge of the 'Tree for All' Campaign, involving the planting of 12 million trees (mostly oaks, says the associated article) covering an area the size 18,000 football pitches, to form some 28 new woods over a planting time period of five years. There is an implied and applaud-able aim of replacing the oaks that were felled to build Nelson's fleet of wooden ships which saved Europe from the 'globalisation' aims of Napoleon. (Perhaps so that our present day politicians could rush to offer GB on a plate to similar aims of other EU enthusiasts, and try to take undue 'credit' for so doing!) Andrew is pictured being surrounded by a multitude of spindly-type off-shoots of Hornbeam (at a guess). However, it is his reported statements that are of more interest here.

The size of a football pitch does not describe a precise area, but such a pitch approximates to 100 metres x 65 metres, which equals 328 feet x 213 feet which amounts to 69864 sq feet. An acre is about 209 x 209 sq feet = 43681 sq feet. It is evident that one football pitch represents 69864/43681 acres = 1.6 acres. (No apologies are tended for utilising Imperial Measurements here!)

Now, 12,000,000 trees on 18,000 football pitches = 667 trees per football pitch AND 667 trees on 1.6 acres = 416 trees per acre, which represents a ten foot spacing between trees.

It follows that since a mature oak will spread its branches to achieve about a 50 feet or so diameter, and since an acre is about 209x209 square feet, one can barely get away with sensible planting (See aims of specialist tree planters, Chapter Eight) of four oak trees per side of a square shaped acre which represents a density of 16 planted trees per acre. The Woodland Trust planting density appears to be 400 trees too many per acre.

The author has written to the Woodland Trust many times on this subject of high density planting and never yet received an explanation of any sort for the practice. This has resulted in great puzzlement, because the oaks that Andrew is planting or has planted will not mature at this stated planting density. And as for replacing the Oaks that built Nelson's fleet, the gentleman will be lucky to get sufficient disease-free timber large enough to build a small dinghy!

The reader might ask: what a charity going about its business got to do with political shortcomings? Well, let's explore the reality. This organisation is part funded by the EU, which, it is believed, means it receives a portion of the current £1.8 million per hour plus, that the British public pays into the EU's unaudited funds. (See Ref 7, a Leaflet issued by United Kingdom Independence Party believed to date from 1998.) (This figure is now much higher, i.e. £1.8 million pounds per hour in 2008, partly because the then Prime Minister, Tony Blair surrendered Right Hon Margaret Thatcher's EU subscription rebate.) And many of the people in GB are struggling to hold down artificially high housing costs (thought to have occurred because implementation of The Town and Country Planning Acts plus the hordes of administering bureaucrats coming together to inhibit the release of sufficient building land) in the form of artificially expensive mortgages. Then there is the potential disease of soil and food crops that will need excessive chemical applications in a bid to hold the status quo.

And what is GB's Government doing about this terrible waste and potential damage? Well, some of its past Ministers, including an ex Environmental Minister, have endorsed the efforts of the Woodland Trust. So it seems there is little doubt that this text is in the right section of this book!

And one begins to see a glimmer of understanding on the subject of the author's vandalised garden!

Storm in a teacup? No way. The author has a file of data given out by the Woodland Trust and it mentions the cost of planting a tree is in the order of £10 sterling per tree. Thinking about it, one has to include Nursery cost, transport costs and administration cost, so the projected cost of £10 a tree might well be reasonable. But I question the cost of 12 million trees at £120 million versus the cost at say 16 trees per acre = £460,000 or, allowing for an excessive 25% loss, £575,000. Added to that figure is the hidden cost of collecting the taxes, inter governmental transfer costs and administration costs of money transfer arrangements to The Woodland Trust! And this projection omits to cost the necessary thinning that may (should) be carried out! This, reader, is one example of where YOUR hard earned cash and taxes go.

And then there are Tree Preservation Orders placed on forest trees growing on high density residential estates. Generalising about this state of affairs, these trees have no real place on such estates. For a start these Preserved Trees rob residents of the little sunlight that may be available after the properties have absorbed the lion's share of the commodity. Added to that problem, there is the danger to which the buildings are exposed from root upheavals to property foundations and drainage systems. (See Ref 6, an extract from a Report issued by Environment Transport Regions Low Rise Buildings, which indicates the influence of trees to building's foundations on clay soils, P3, Table 1, attached, copyright BRE reproduced by kind permission of BRE from Digest 298, Low Rise Building Foundations.) For example, a Poplar tree under stated conditions* can cause damage to foundations at distances of 60 feet or more! I await ETR's Report that deals with the same aspect of danger to building foundations on non-clay soils! The law regarding the rights of the owner or tenant with regard to danger to the person, damage from tree roots and blocked sunlight are patently unaffordable and painfully inadequate. Admittedly, some steps were recently taken by Parliament with regard to the control of Leyland ii trees or hedges which grow extremely tall very quickly indeed. But they have given the unnecessary costly control (see Ref 5 Article 12 re recommendations) of these powers to the LAs, which are the same people that vandalised the author's garden in the 70s!

* The water take up by tree roots dries out the clay soil resulting in shrinkage of this commodity ....leaving unsupported property foundations in a position of peril from collapse!

Further unwarranted interferences come from people in high places who, along with the Government quangos, unilaterally decide to dictate Residential Housing Policies without recourse to the people. One such example was reported in The Express dated 12 Feb'07 (See Writer's letter dated 12 Feb '07 to the *Daily Express* Ref 16), and places the Cul-de-Sac under threat from at least one influential character who is thought to live in a specialised Cul-De-Sac himself. All of the foregoing seems to bestow betrayal of the first order, since it is obvious one cannot successfully surrender the control of any asset to a third party.

Then there is the example of Mrs Molley, the old age pensioner from Eastbourne who requested and was refused permission from the LA, namely the Eastbourne Borough Council, to fell forest trees which were considered dangerous just four weeks before they crashed into her house during a storm. The house was badly damaged and the lady and her husband (who subsequently died of a heart attack) had to be led to safety from the wreckage of her house by the police. And the Council then required her to replace the fallen trees, which were subject to, yes, you've guessed it, a TREE PRESERVATION ORDER. (Ref 2 Attached, Eastbourne Herald Oct 16th '93). Of course, the officials involved are still on course to receive salary increases and full inflation-proofed pensions.

(It is a very relevant question to ask why this is so in view of the foregoing text.) And the Government response to the disclosed events is...zero! That is, the Law stands as it was prior to the occurrences. IT'S TIME TO WAKE UP PARLIAMENTARIANS and DO THE JOB YOU WERE ELECTED TO DO.

I call again for the re-write of the Town & Country Planning Acts in view of the fact that there are people who seem oblivious to, or perhaps even enjoy, the inconvenience, damage, destruction and even death or severe injury that they cause to others through growing, nurturing or ignoring the danger presented by misplaced forest trees. And they are assisted by Parliament's unbalanced and lax legislation such as Tree Preservation Orders and inadequate redress laws resulting from ignorance or bloody-minded behaviour. The author also backs the call (See Ref 3, Attached, Birmingham Mail dated 13th August, 2001) for prosecution of persons exercising lax behaviour such as owners, MPs or Officials when siting, nurturing or ignoring the danger presented by irresponsible saving of trees. There are also suggestions (See Ref 4, Attached, CLASSICAL ENVIRONMENTAL FOLLY ED 5 1992) and (Ref 5 Attached, 'A PROPOSAL FOR A WRITTEN CONSTITUTION ISS 3 Dated JAN '07)' for the revision of the Town and Country Planning Acts that would take care of the required protection for the public against the unacceptable occurrences exposed in all of the foregoing text, IF implemented.

Additions to Issue 2 of this edition

The Author has also added the final correspondence to the Ombudsman in the Appendix which is dated 28th April 2014 plus 10 photographs [see Reference 18 in Issue 2 of this book Page 162] after more than ten years correspondence with the authorities concerning the parking of cars, van & lorries & the existence of Forest Trees in Mossman Drive & Holly Farm Close boundary, where the author lives. It is not clear to the author if the Authorities are fully aware that there should be zero Forest Trees on building sites situated on a clay bed.

Although the issue is not yet officially accepted, [November 2014] necessary changes in parking of vehicles has partly occurred in Mossman Drive where the author lives. This however, is inadequate, since a referendum has been held regarding Mossman Drive rules re: parking & it is imperative that this matter is officially adopted in due course by the Council....since it was considered a necessity by the Council in 1996 in the Planning Approval of the Building Plan.

However, the scheme was not finally accepted at a following Council Meeting for reasons that are not understood! But vehicles are still intermittently parking on both sides of Mossman Drive entrance {& outside the writers garage]. And it is presenting a great danger....since there have been three accidents due to parking in this driveway to the limited knowledge of the writer.

And there is still no change regarding the removal of five Forest Trees to date [November 2014] ....apart from one tree having its top trimmed. This act is irrelevant as it doesn't affect the peril to vulnerable property foundations. [See Reference 6 in the Appendix} The reason for this failure is, say the Council, because the writer's house is situated too far from the Forest Trees. But the kerbside in Mossman Drive is photographed housing thousands of Forest Tree seeds. {see reference 18 photographs] Furthermore, the writer has removed some sixty Forest Tree Saplings from the 24 foot long hedge situated fifteen feet from the writer's property's front door. And it is obvious the situation needs fundamental Parliamentary change. And then there are other peoples gardens to consider!

Also, earlier this year [2014] Nina Hossain announced on the 1800hrs ITV News Broadcast that the Gulf Stream had reduced its speed of flow. Further, [& in 2014] Prof: Hawkin of Cambridge University, UK announced on line that by looking into space [presumably with the Hubble Telescope} that it was discovered that there were two explosions separated by a few milliseconds in the 'BIG BANG' that formed our Galaxy, The Milky Way. Both these facts were properly reported in International Political & Environmental Folly Issue 1 published in the United States of America in 2011. And the fact that there were two explosions in the period of THE BIG BANG is covered in some detail by the earth bound investigation in the content of the original issue & again in the second Edition of International Political & Environmental Folly.

Additions to Chapter 8 Issue 3

Additionally, The Daily Mail, on Saturday, November 1st, 2014, reported Britain is now paying 11.3bn Pounds per annum [plus the extra demand of the EU of 1.7bn Pounds] into the EU's UNAUDITED master fund.

And then there is the 12bn Pounds 'aid' given to various European Countries which is apparently being handed out to thieves, dictators & charlatons, reported in the Mail, dated Sunday 7th June, 2015. Added to that, in the same Edition of the Mail, there is the UK's 1 Billion Pounds spent on 'wood chips' from the USA to burn in the Drax Power Station, which is described as a waste, because the burnt chips are said to be producing more greenhouse emissions than the 'source' emitted as a coal burning generating plant.

Thus the reported 26bn Pounds are being 'blown' abroad.... without the writer even digging for the information.....revealing what it is thought NOT to be a final figure.

One should not neglect to mention & thank, the Chancellor of the Exchequer, who has culled 4bn Pounds of funding to UK Citizens in June 2015...a figure which was dynamically increased to 12bn Pounds...... and which may have been necessary. But what is holding a further 26bn Pounds being saved when we, as a Nation, are up to our eyeballs in debit?...[Apart from agreements, which need cancelling.]

Just what our Political leader are doing about these outrages I do not know. But we should, in my opinion, be acting responsibly with this reported waste & finally start preparing to leave the EU ASAP... as Greece appears about to do.....and restore the ability of 'The Man In The Street' to attend Parliament to report on other matters that appear not to be in keeping with the interets of the British Public.

Additions to Chapter 8 Issue 5 dated July 2017

One can hardley ignore the issues apparently affecting approximately 500 of GB's Multi Story Residential Blocks & the inability of these buildings to stand up to minor outbreaks of fire as experienced in London in 2017.

Apparently, this London mishap was the result of an oversight on the part of a Local Authority....an oversight which apparently was duplicated throughout the UK. The error consisted of cladding the London Building with an aluminium coating which 'sandwiched' an inflamable plastic substance. This error caused an' inferno' which more or less destroyed the multi story building from the result of a minor outbreak of fire believed caused by a faulty fridge freezer.

Subsequent investigations have revealed 80 deaths due to this out of control inferno. And tests throughout the Country have revealed 200 High Rise Residential Blocks are suffering from the same faulty cladding material that caused this London outrage! The remaining 300 Tower Blocks are being investigated, but to my knowledge, no Official Reports have been issued re: the findings of this further investigation. This maybe because the investigations are not complete. But it is believed the insultion behind the aluminium sandwhich cladding is found a thermal cladding ......which is, in many if not all cases, to be composed of a further inflamable material.

It would seem that overall life is becoming too complicated & expensive to leave complex saftey rules in the hands of many hard working folk who take up the responsibilities of Council & other Political work...And it maybe time to consider fresh approaches to Public safety.

Perhaps the Public should be left to proceed with 'projects' which are controlled by written measures [e g, as outlined in this Book.] employing safety procedures.....with severe penalties for 'overstepping' permitted actions without requesting auhorisation & obtaining permission to do so. Beside helping to regain a balance economy, the resultant reduced expenditure may make it easier to finance repositioning of the Solar System.'

NINE
More Political Shortcomings

It is difficult task to pin blame on to any individual politician for unacceptable behaviour with regard to policy because their work is fragmented, that is, a bit is done here and a bit done there.

Also the politicians are well protected by the laws they pass. So, pinning the blame on whomsoever is responsible for run-away council tax charges is almost impossible. None the less the author thinks the runaway financial situation was, and still is, being orchestrated by bureaucrats and the objectionable act is being permitted by some parliamentarians.

So the best that can be done with a situation of this nature is to expose the detail to officials who are in a position to do something about the scandal. And that means informing ones MP and the Prime Minister, as well as bureaucrats - which is just what the author did, and the resultant action was zero. So the only other option is to expose the matter to the media and finally the Fraud Squad, and these attempts to remedy the situation failed too. Maybe they are all 'in it' together!

Few would argue with the suggestion that the situation with regard to Local Authority taxation is out of control, unaffordable, unnecessary and not fit for purpose or presents value for money. As said earlier, it is also fundamentally incorrect to give third parties control of another's assets. So, if the Parliamentarians ignore this sort of behaviour and the related escalation in cost, it reveals the disgusting level to which our Parliamentary system has sunk. And it signals the end of GB because a proportion of these MPs, perhaps the unprincipled members, will, it seems, give everything the country or its people hold dear or that gives independent control over destiny or belongings....to UK or EU bureaucrats!.

The only solution is fundamental corrective action of the political scene. And the only ploy open to the man in the street to save GB from becoming a 'dependant appendage' to the EU and UK bureaucrats appears to be in exposure of the sell-out and hope that the electorate will grasp the opportunity presented to force changes through the use of selective voting at the ballot box. And this means a determined effort, because the system, yes, THE SYSTEM, is currently held together by cash handouts of our taxes and some advantaged politicians JOCKEYING FOR LUCRATIVE POSITIONS WITHIN THE EU. That means excessive amounts of cash for salaries, expenses, pensions, welfare, feigned immobility and whatever else you care to think of to all and sundry, so clearly, the correction regarding this exposure of what is really taking place will certainly be an uphill struggle.

However, it appears possible to show that the ex Prime Minister and his Deputy were well aware, or should have been well aware, of the sickening exposure that is to follow. I refer to the author's Report entitled 'A REPORT REQUESTING PARLIAMENT FOR COUNCIL TAX REDUCTIONS' dated NOVEMBER '98. (See Ref 8, Attached). This Report was widely circulated to the then Prime Minister, MPs, Councillors, Council Chief Executives, Resident Association Chairmen and the Fraud Squad, all to no avail.

The Report shows the Rate/Poll Tax/Council Tax from inception (1959) to 1998 of a Tax Band D Dorset bungalow, situated in the Borough of Christchurch. This property was bought by the author as a retirement retreat in 1985. As mentioned previously, its initial local tax was £25 per annum and that included the Sewage disposal charge. By 1998 this had escalated to £850 sterling and the Sewage charges had been transferred to a Third Party without a corresponding reduction in council tax demands being apparent, and that amounted to a 3600% increase over the period under discussion, versus the RPI escalation of 550%!

This highly imaginative form of 'Accounting' was termed 'double charging' by the author. And there were more examples of this unacceptable practice uncovered as the Report was compiled. The police service cost Dorset County Council £64 Million per annum until it was decided that the Constabulary was to issue each Local Council with a proportionate charge. The expected result of this reported change was that the DCC budget would decrease by £64 million, but no such decrease occurred. The actual decrease amounted to some £13 Million! And of course, the local taxpayer still had to fund the Police. As already stated, the outgoings (comparing like with like, which precludes the use of the word 'tax') during the period covered from '59 to '98 to the owners of said Dorset bungalow was increased by some 3600% compared to the RPI of about 550% and the increases still continue. To complete the picture, the charges on this band D property for this financial year (2008) was £1,480, plus sewage charges of £274 and water charge of £175, totalling some £1,929!

It is thought the unsavoury practice was adopted in principle throughout GB since the general level of local Property Tax remained and remains very similar throughout the whole Country. Taking exposures of the Report a step further (the Reader can explore the finer points by referring to Ref 8) there are more examples of this dubious Accounting practice that was perpetrated by Westminster in connection with this Local Tax scandal.

When the Poll Tax was instituted, the amount of tax demand doubled in many households. This produced a roar of disapproval from the public, and Prime Minister John Major of the day, who inherited the problem from the Right Hon Margaret Thatcher administration, is thought to have asked The Right Honourable Gentleman Micheal Heseltine to sort the matter out. As a result, a refund was granted householders to reduce outgoings to somewhere nearer, but at a higher figure than hitherto. The Local Councils now squealed they had been robbed and Central Government are reported to have put the cost of Value Added Tax up by 2.5% in order to fund the Local Authority demand.

Subsequently the local taxes carried on rising until it exceeded the amount that caused the initial public outcry. But the VAT increase of 2.5 % remain to this very day (2008 and further unrelated increase were imposed in 2011) and one need not be a Chartered Accountant to realise that we, the public, appear to have been double-charged yet again.

When these outrageous 'goings on' are added to the £1.8 million sterling per hour, yes, PER HOUR, paid to EU unaudited accounts to settle costs of our unauthorised EU Membership or more, since PM Tony Blair surrendered the Ex Prime Minister Margaret Thatcher's EU rebate, without it must be said, any tangible concession being received from the Brussel's regime, one has a right to raise one's eyebrows at the very least! Particularly since the EU accounts have been refused approval by its Auditing Body for some fourteen consecutive years. And one mustn't forget Lord N. Kinnock's reported part in this sordid and disgusting affair. But the situation wants more than mere raised eyebrows: IT NEEDS Political REFORM with a CAPITAL 'R'.

To continue, it was reported at the time that the entire EU Commissioners resigned from their lucrative EU posts because there were awkward questions over the EU accounts that were not answered. Lord Kinnock was reported as being re-appointed as EU Commissioner to sort the matter out. A whistle-blower in the form of The EC Commissioners Chief Accountant, Martha

Andreasen, who working under Commissioner Kinnock, raised her head above the parapet to reveal suspected fraud and was summarily dismissed from her post for breach of trust. The matter is reported in some detail by Quentin Letts in the *Daily Mail* dated 2nd Feb '05 who says that her grossly unfair dismissal had Lord Kinnock's fingerprints all over the act. In other words, it appears that fraud and theft of huge sums of money went into thin air without corrective action or actual charges or court proceeding taking place which might pin blame on any individual because…?

In case the reader thinks this may be just another storm in a teacup, the Audit Commission is reported by Mr Letts as revealing that waste doubled to £700 million a year under the auspices of Commissioner, now Lord Kinnock. And the cases of corruption uncovered, but apparently not dealt with, amounted to 10,000 in number! The *News of the World* & the *Mail on Sunday* reported on the 12 June 2009 that Lord and Lady Kinnock received some £8 million to £10 million salary, expenses and allowances during their time as EU employees - some might think that is an excessive amount even if we, the public, have been well served by such highly paid representatives!

TEN
Continuation of Political Shortcomings

The evidence to support the belief that the then Prime Minister Tony Blair and possibly his Deputy, John Prescott, were aware of the issuing of 'A Report Requesting Parliament for Council Tax Reductions' (Ref 8, Attached,] comes from letters dated 9th Dec '98, [See Ref 11] from the Office of Mr B. Entwistle - this same gentleman also wrote to the author on 12th Nov 2002 (See Ref 10) from the Deputy Prime Minister's Office), so it is reasonable to suppose DPM Prescott was also aware of the author's Report, REF 8.

The third paragraph of the letter dated 12th Nov '02 indicates that reserve capping powers would only be used in exceptional circumstances, and in light of said Report, Ref 8, and my letter to M Moran and the PM dated 22nd Dec '02, Ref 9, revealing that the percentage increase in LA annual Taxation increases were greater than the maximum amount expected by central government for the period as portrayed by Mr B. Entwhistle's letter, Ref 11, one would ask what would the Government of the day (or any day) consider to be 'exceptional circumstances'?

Reverting to this same gentleman's letter of 9th Dec '98, Ref 11, his paragraph 4 states the Government expected, and apparently would tolerate, Council Tax rises for the following three years of up to 4.5% per annum, which included an allowance for inflation (In view of exposed increases that went before; one has to ask why this was so?) But paragraph 4 of my letter dated 22 Dec '02 (See Ref 9, Attached) to Prime Minister and MP Ms M Moran appears to show that the annual tax demands of at least one LA were on average 8% up during the period the Government expected 4.5% increase; maximum. The attitude of the Government of that day which directly seems to involve DPM

John Prescott and PM Tony Blair appears to be 'pacify the mob' and let things run their intended course. This is an unacceptable situation from our elected representatives whom, it appears, were aware of the situation...a situation which had been running for some time, completely out of control, according to Central Government's stated guidelines. AND THEY, the powers that be, DID NOTHING ABOUT CORRECTING EXPOSED MATTERS! Furthermore, apart from the fact that they ignored reasoned request for necessary restraining action to address the situation, the matter under discussion appears to be out of control to this very day. [2009]

Adding to the disgusting state of affairs exposed in this Chapter the author reproduces three letters [Ref 12] showing three two line acknowledgement letters, absolutely identical in content apart from the date, which emanated from then PM Tony Blair's Office dated Feb 8th , 16th February and 7th April, all 1999. A further example of letters which seemed to indicate the same careless attitude toward members of the public concerns as the letters received from Mr B Entwistle - letters which were not acted upon positively and did not react to the request for control of unreasonable and unacceptable LA's Tax demands.

It is also reported that a hand-written note was found by detectives during the recent 'investigation into Honours for Cash' that directly linked the then Prime Minister, Tony Blair, to the scandal. The revelation raises the question as to why prosecution of those involved did not following the indepth investigation.

Then there is a report detailing £500 billion spend by Tony Blair's Government which did not appear on the Treasury Expenditure Accounts, which was Prime Minister G Brown's department at the time. The matter was artificially reduced in importance because the payments for Capital Expenditure such as in schools and hospitals was spread over a period of years. Thus the expenditure became a day to day Treasury Expense, although the item that caused the biggest dent in this unacceptable Accounting method was Civil Servants' pensions. This item would account for a large proportion of the Gross Domestic Product if it were included in the Government's balance sheet. To complete the picture, the scale of Public Debt is reported as £1,100 billion sterling in February 2007.

Furthermore it was reported at the time of these occurrences that Right Hon Jack Straw altered the rules controlling the already generous pension pot-size paid to ex Ministers. The said alteration would apparently increase the already huge amount of 'pension pot' supposed to be due (the author thinks that point is debatable) to Right Hon John Prescott, Deputy Prime Minister.

A further act of treachery against the British People is reported on 14th Dec '91, where, on that very day, the Prime Minister signed a document giving EU judges a right to issue an arrest warrant on a British subject on British soil on a possible 'trumped up charge' over laws which do not necessarily exist in the UK. And the arrest will be carried out with no Consular or Court Protection or rights whatever for the unfortunate individual.

This act of a single man, Tony Blair, who as Prime Minister was answerable to Parliament, apparently single-handedly threw away the 800 year old protection of the Magna Charta's Habeas Corpus, and the Home Office says MPs cannot even debate the matter until February, weeks after the shameful deed was signed into being. Terrorism, which is the flimsy excuse for the deed, needs to be stamped out but one questions if this is the way forward and warns the man in the street that what happened to the Greek plane-spotters is how one stands to be treated. This is because apparently in many EU Countries a jailed man doesn't need to be charged and tried in a Court of Law within a given time period or, alternatively, be released, but can be jailed indefinitely. The author thinks the perpetrator of this disgusting affair, which seems to bode ill for fair minded criticism of our Lords and Masters, should be impeached for that single act alone.

And yet another example of questionable accounting practice is reported in 2006 which seems to show Bedfordshire County Council underspent its budget projections by some £8 million. This report, dear reader, then indicates the stated underspend was then placed into Council Reserves, i.e. money taken as tax was stored for another unspecified use instead of being returned to the tax payer. Attempts to verify the reported matter were not successful but further reading may be obtainable from Luton and Dunstable Times dated June 14th 2006.

More serious examples of putting public money to council Reserves is believed to have occurred in the UK regarding funds raised from council house sales to the Housing Association in the 1980's.

Some UK councils' seem to have taken advantage of massive house price inflation....sold their council housing stock at a profit , and cleared debts. They then put sizeable financial gain to their reserves but did not reduce their local tax demands. These actions would seem to leave the man in the street with higher repayments to clear the new and larger loans ....plus the need to support an increased number public servants. If an accurate assessment, a smart but unacceptable operation by an overhead organisation such as Local Government is ...because it appears to have used an underhand way of transferring enormous funding from the over burdened taxpayer to Council funds. If legal, such Accountancy should be made illegal....and some form of redress should be applied! Because that, dear reader, is YOUR MONEY being taken as tax and put into COUNCIL RESERVES, where it will probably be blown on some pet folly harboured by councillors, who ought to be restrained by law from these kind of practices!

The current 2009 Global Economic Downturn is blamed by the Political Set on the lax lending of the Banking World, but true as that may be in part, the bad debit situation has been caused, especially in the USA, by 'the man in in the street' mass failure to service mortgage loans for housing. The inability of borrowers to pay these and other debts might also be due to the massive waste and cost of local and national Government, on an international scale That is, the public cannot afford these excessive government overheads and at the same time pay for personal necessities of life. Most Governments would appear to be at fault here, and ought to be made to radically scale down their excessive tax demands.

Added to the foregoing there is the then Prime Minister of the UK reported as declaring that he was 'wanting to Rule all Europe' It prompts the question: Were Britain's affairs being managed to suit Tony Blair's personal plans? A lot of his Government's mysterious policies would seem to have had a much more sensible basis (from his point of view) if one assumes that the answer to the previous question is affirmative. The possible repercussions of such an occurrence for the UK so alarmed the author that it prompted the document 'A NOTE TO THE BRITISH PEOPLE' dated Nov 29 '04 Ref 13, attached. The note to the Public might not have been in vain if the lessons of this work are given credence and acted upon by the British Public.

The other thing that appears to separate the Political Set from their constituents is that 'establishment' offenders rarely get taken to Court to answer for their wrong-doings and on the rare occasions when they are taken to task they are NOT usually , as the man in the street defending his nearest and dearest or property, treated harshly enough to deter. The reverse is true for the general public and I cite cases of 80 year old pensioners jailed for protesting against the 'robber barons' - who set our unaffordable local taxes, by withholding Council Tax 'DUES'. Also consider the case of jailed Tony Martin who surprised, shot and killed an intruder in or about to enter, or leave, his isolated home after sundown. The author does not know the intruders intent that night. It may have been robbery or intent to maim or even murder the resident gentleman. Even if murder was not the intent, who knows what may happen when detection or identification of the intruder is established.

Remember, there would be little or no help from the people paid to protect us who were probably busy arresting old age pensioners who failed to pay their Council Tax!

To be fair, our 'Political Masters' did finally say it is ok to defend ones assets 'providing reasonable force is used', and at the same time uttering a refusal to change the law in favour of the wronged citizen! * How can one be expected to use reasonable force when one's home is invaded in the depth of the night or even in broad daylight. The action taken would be in response to need and involuntary released supplies of adrenaline, and the offenders are the intruders and should put up with whatever is dished out in the heat of the moment, including death. It is time the Law was properly amended to reflect the suggested changes.

* Brave words & a completely inadequate response from our representatives, many of whom receive round the clock ARMED police protection!

The Tony Martin case is not unique. There is also the case of 72-year-old Daniel Taylor who lived alone in an isolated dwelling. His property was invaded some 60 times in all. Imagine the fear of going to bed wondering if there would be a repeat session at, say, midnight. Anyway the police, who often remain above being called upon to protect life and property, took away his shotgun. So Daniel remained alone and unarmed for the last six years of his life, which ended in 1996 when the final intruder stabbed the defenceless old chap to death with a screwdriver! Meanwhile, the police were probably arguing about their pension rights or were busy copping motorists exceeding the speed limit by one mile an hour! So, let's get the law amended to deal with these cases in an even handed way which apply to ALL people, including criminals, politicians and police too!

A word also about the non-hanging policy in the cases of Court proven murder utilising DNA technology. This particular failing by the State appears to the author, taken account of in isolation, bad enough, but appears to be made into an intolerable situation by allowing Police Officers to 'shoot-to-kill' people who are THOUGHT to be Terrorists or armed, sometimes mistakenly, without trial or redress! Again it appears the State has one rule for its 'own' and another rule for 'the man in the street'. And the chumps who commission, formulate and legislate such nonsensical and intolerable bunkum are, in the author's eyes, thought not to be fit for purpose!

The extent of GB's decline and the prospect of terminal decline appears to be revealed in a letter dated 12th Feb '07 (See Ref 15, Attached) to Right Hon David Cameron, the then leader of the Opposition. It seems to show what GB is faced with in reality regarding the EU and what our political leaders are doing, or are not doing, with regard to this threat. Well, lets not mince words....their actions appear as inappropriate at worst just plain pathetic at best, since the man in the street has not been given the opportunity to accept or reject the matter of affiliation to the EU! One thing is clear to the author and that is that GB's INTERESTS DO NOT APPEAR TO BE WELL SERVED.

This chapter may be considered incomplete unless a mention is made of MP's scandalous Expenses ado (See Newspaper reports in 2009/2010) and what seems like excessive salaries for politicians in general when weighed against performances reported within this work.

ELEVEN
Analysis, Conclusions and Solutions

The time has now come to decide whether or not this work has substance, i.e. to analyse the foregoing. From this vantage point we can further decide if we accept the findings, form conclusions and apply solutions.

The author has no doubt that the work has substance. Having spent fifty something years battling against the IMPOSED rotten and faulty system, not because of cussedness, but because of experienced vandalism, coupled with unaffordable and fiddled costs associated with said vandalism. Additionally, a representation system that is always stating that further assistance is available, but the obvious (to the author at any rate) need for changes simply rarely occur, all of which raises the matter of efficiency and honesty issues with GB's people from a system that we should have faith in.

In fact, at times in the past, it seemed as though the system was deliberately steering OUR country down paths that were fundamentally incorrect to oppose the logic put out by alarmed observers. This trait was particularly noticeable under the auspices of the Blair regime... If correctly sized up, THE SYSTEM seemed to generally display the symptoms of immature minds at work. Instead, it may have been reflecting devious minds at work, feathering their own nests and settling national scores at the same time. Whatever, it has almost wrecked GB and has nearly reached the point of no return.

However late in the day it may be as far as damaging progress has proceeded, the point of 'no return' has not yet been reached in the author's humble opinion. And it is up to the 'MAN IN STREET' to insist that the political system reverses these disastrous policies that have been exposed in the forgoing

Chapters, always assuming that the majority of the UK population agree with the logic and believe that the actions presented are unacceptable....and most certainly not in the national interest! After all, surely no home-owner would willingly part with what little control is left over his home, be it a humble cottage or large country estate, so why tolerate the imposed imposition whether the axiom applies to one's home or one's country! Failure to address the situation with regard to one's country may be tantamount to becoming a 'stateless person' building mere 'castles in the sand'!

Clearly, if the reader accepts the foregoing paragraph then the next step is to look for solutions to the problem, which falls short of a civil war or armed insurrection; that is, to decide if the Political Machine presently in place needs proper public administered control. And IF the decision is that it does need controlling, IT CAN BE DONE, MY FRIENDS.

'How?' Well, as Noel Edmonds has said *We Can Make a Difference Too*, each of us has to do a little bit. This is not a battle of the 'Lefties' versus the 'Righties'....it's a battle to put some backbone into our SERVANTS, the Political Force. This Force, which although it purports to offer some three different approaches to Government appears to be fundamentally in agreement that we are on the 'right road'. This is not a statement that the leaders of our three main parties have issued - it is a summary of what they seem to stand for and one that their fine oratory cannot disguise, where GB's interests appear, intentionally or neglectfully, far down the list, I am sorry to say.

The fight has to begin RIGHT NOW. Make it clear to your Political Association's Chairman, your MP, your local & National Press Editors that you will not vote for parliamentary candidates who do not promise to adhere to policies which take us out of Europe and re-establish complete national control of our nation's affairs. We must declare that we want to fundamentally reform our abused Town and Country Planning Acts on the lines laid down in the foregoing text & reports, as well as totally reforming our abused welfare system, reducing waste and local and national taxation levels.

Hang on just a minute more before making a decision - think what a nation could provide by way of UK well-being if its systems were efficiently run and we got the £1.8 million or more per hour of EU imposed funding from the British taxpayer's plate.

NB RT Hon George Osborne's emerging budget [2010] and EU directives or comments brought to light the prospect of delaying GB's OAP payments till the recipient reaches seventy years of age. Why is this so when large amounts of GB's EU dues [about £1.8 million per hour] are being freely scattered among hordes of EU politicians and their supporting bureaucrats as salaries, perks and pensions ....in return for what?

We would not need to lose trade if the Unilateral Independence Agreement was to be negotiated by a resolved politician. And resolved he would be if he realised that a large percentage of the population would not vote or maintain support for a feeble negotiator like many of our present political leaders appear to be!

Furthermore, Trade does not depend upon favours. It depends on REQUIRED GOODS BEING DELIVERED ON TIME AT THE RIGHT PRICE, and with huge amounts of wasted tax removed from our national load , our goods would become VERY COMPETITIVE without the workforce SUFFERING the LOSS of ONE penny. In fact, commercial success brings HIGHER REWARDS TO ALL!

All it requires to achieve this necessary goal is three or four letters from each dedicated Briton, and surely saving OUR NATION is worth that tiny effort. You might, if and when you are a 100% EU 'SLAVE' realise the sense that last sentence makes much more readily than now where the EU System is merely nibbling at the edges of your world, disruptive as that might be! It is thought to be clear that more control needs to be exercised over our UK Political elite and one of the more direct approaches would be to insist that the Written Constitution, See Ref 5, be implemented with particular emphasise on Article 13, Clause 38.

But there appears to be yet another fundamental flaw that prevents political opposition or action from an elected MP. The political associations select and assist MPs in their election campaigns, but they may also unwittingly provide a platform for an individual member to exert undue influence or pressure. In most constituencies there is a well-known and sometimes pleasant man who can fix anything. He is usually well entrenched in the LA and every other sphere where power is wielded.

And I have heard a Treasurer of one local organisation say: 'Yes, you are quite right, the matter needs attention, but I can't do anything to help or I may lose my coveted post!' It seems to me that an MP may be under a similar threat if he or she tried to do something about reducing LA powers, for example, even though the matter requiring attention is obviously dubious or even obviously in need of correction ...as with the exposures that have been aired in the foregoing text.

If an MP crosses the line of such an influential character, the conclusions the author has reached is that de-selection of that MP may follow. The author is not sure what can be done to stop the possibility or prospect of such paralysing situations arising, but the matter seems to need serious corrective action of some sort, so that where the practice exists, it is completely inhibited. It just may be that these political organisations should, by law, be required to obtain an MP's selection or de selection vote from at least 50% of unaffiliated public voting rights!

The foregoing is a timely warning to the citizens of this globe of ours whose political 'Masters' have taken note of the highly lucrative lifestyle that globalisation can bring to participating politicians and stop the rot in its tracks before it produces the unaffordable state that GB finds itself in. These politicians are our servants, and whereas they should be treated with respect, that respect has to be earned, and that means the majority requirement has to be considered. Remember, Turkeys* don't vote for Christmas!

* A Turkey is a traditional UK Christmas dinner.

And I can hear some busy Nationals saying 'why bother, it doesn't bother me that much'. Well, it will, my friends. And action left until the 'KEY IS TURNED IN THE LOCK' is unwise 'cos it will prove very, very, very difficult to turn the key in the reverse direction! All it requires is three or four letters from each voter.

And finally, we bother to build a house, we bother to cook food, we bother to shave and wash, we bother to grow food, we bother to go to work if we can find a job...ALL BECAUSE IT IS WORTH IT...AND SO TOO IS CORRECT AND INDEPENDENT GOVERNMENT WORTH THE BOTHERING TO RESTORE, TEND and CULTIVATE.

Sadly my friends, many of our well paid politicians have a different agenda and focus to their constitutions and are intent on harnessing YOUR efforts to achieve their goals. IF you are prepared to permit the occurrence of such a treacherous outrage, it means, in effect, relegation of your nation. Relegation of a nation occurs when its indigenous population fails, for whatever reason, to uphold its rightful ability to manage its own affairs. And, if proof is needed, just look at the present plight of the indigenous populations of North and South America, the peoples of Africa and the original occupants of New Zealand and Australia.

GOOD BYE and GOOD LUCK to each of you.

APPENDIX.

Reference 1 is reproduced by kind permission Woodland Trust.

Reference 2 is reproduced by kind permission of Eastbourne Herald.

Reference 3 is reproduced by kind permission of Birmingham Mail.

Reference 6 is reproduced by kind permission of BRE from Digit 298 Low Rise Building Foundations.

Reference 7 is reproduced by kind permission of UK Independence Party.

References 10/11/12 are reproduced & licenced under Open Government Licence v1.0.

Reference 18 is reproduced to comply with requirements of Issue 2 of International Political & Environmental Folly.

REF 1

Andrew Beer the tree planter

At least a million people, many of them children, will be involved in the huge tree-planting project being masterminded by Andrew Beer. The aim is to plant 12 million trees over five years, covering an area the size of 18,000 football pitches.

Andrew, 36, a conservationist and campaigner with the Woodland Trust, is in charge of the "Tree For All" campaign. His target of 12 million trees represents one for every youngster under 16 in Britain, and some of the trees – mostly oaks – will be grouped to form 28 new woods, each of which will be named after one of Nelson's battleships. For the past year, Andrew has been touring the country persuading landowners to devote or even donate valuable acres for planting. The response has been so overwhelming that another five Trafalgar Woods are to be added.

From Ajax Wood in Co Durham to Dreadnought in Co Down, from Perthshire to Cornwall, all will be planted with knee-high, year-old saplings. Children have already planted hundreds of oaks overlooking the Solent, traditional home waters of the Royal Navy, but the prime site is the wood to be named after Nelson's flagship. It will occupy 350 acres between Canterbury and Faversham, Kent.

"In the national euphoria following Trafalgar, landowners were encouraged to grow new hedgerows, copses and plantations to mark the victory. These trees have survived and we want today's generation to appreciate that heritage," says Andrew. "It has been utterly inspiring. Children immediately grasp the importance of what we're doing. They realise that they will never see the full fruits of their efforts, yet they understand that what they are creating will be here for another 1,000 years."
www.woodland-trust.org.uk

June 2005

REF 2

Eastbourne Herald, Satu

MP SLAMS 'SLEDGEHAMMER TO CRACK NUT' ENFORCEMENT ACTION

Row over OAP's 'Act of God' bill

EASTBOURNE HERALD Oct 16 1993

MOLLY Davidson with MP Nigel Waterson beside one of the new trees she has planted in her garden at her own cost.

MRS DAVIDSON and her husband had to be led to safety after the 60ft trees crashed onto their home during the 1987 hurricane.

A 73-YEAR-OLD pensioner is taking on council chiefs who insist she replaces trees blown down in the '87 hurricane.

Mrs Molly Davidson and her husband had to be led to safety by police after four 60ft trees fell onto their home during the October 16 storm.

But her nightmare has continued because the borough council wants Mrs Davidson to replace those trees.

Ironically she and her husband, who died shortly afterwards of a heart attack, had asked the council a month

By Jane Gould

before the storm to remove the trees because they thought them dangerous.

The council refused because the trees were covered by preservation orders.

For the next four years Mrs Davidson heard nothing from the council.

She replaced a damaged fence at a cost of £1,200, and planted 17 Lawson Cypress trees to form a hedge inside the fence — costing a further £280.

Notice

But on October 18 1991 an enforcement notice was pushed through the letterbox of her Shortlands Close home, requiring her to replace the trees.

Since then Mrs Davidson has been locked in a bitter wrangle with the borough council.

But she is not alone in the fight having recruited the support of Ratton ward councillor Mrs Barbara Goodall and Eastbourne MP Nigel Waterson.

'I just thought it was absolutely ridiculous. Apart from the fact I

didn't know we had to put them back, I didn't see why I should replace them at my expense when they were blown down by an act of God,' Mrs Davidson said.

Under the Town and Country Planning Acts of 1971 and 1990, Mrs Davidson is obliged to replace trees of 'appropriate size and species.'

The only tree the council does find acceptable is a maple tree planted in memory of her husband.

Mrs Davidson's solicitor, Glen Stone, has lodged an appeal against the notice.

He has asked the Department of the Environment to determine whether the notice is valid.

MP Nigel Waterson said the council was using 'a sledgehammer to crack a nut.'

'Mrs Davidson is hardly responsible for the hurricane, and I would have thought council officers could find better things to do with their time. This is a case where the law, as operated by Eastbourne Borough Council, is an ass,' Mr Waterson said.

Mr Martin Ray, borough solicitor, said they too were waiting for a decision by the DoE.

REF 3

Evening Mail

www.icbirmingham.co.uk   MONDAY, AUGUST 13, 2001   32p

TREE DEATHS ACTION CALL

Aftershave 'car bomb' creates a real stink

■ AFTERMATH: Emergency services at the scene of the tragedy and, inset, victim Alan Poole   Picture by Kirsty Wigglesworth

Bring those responsible to court - lawyer

By Jane Tyler and Caroline Wheeler

SOLICITORS acting for the widow of a man who died in a triple death tragedy when a tree was blown on to cars today called for anyone found responsible be prosecuted.

Legal representatives acting for Sandra Davis, the widow of Kenneth Davis, also called for the Government to speed-up legislation to make such prosecutions possible.

Alison Fahy, of Thompsons Solicitors, made the call as an inquest into the deaths opened in Birmingham. She said: "Just as company directors get away scot free when their employees are killed at work, it is a disgrace that no-one has been held responsible for the deaths of three members of the public."

Mr Davis's elderly mother, Ellen, and another motorist, Alan Poole, were the other victims.

The call was backed by Mrs Davis, who said: "No amount of compensation will make up for losing two people who were

● **TURN TO PAGE 2**

"Traffic was diverted as the 'bomb' detonated, leaving a gaping hole in the man's boot.

Insp Isherwood said: "It turned out the parcel contained aftershave and was from three of the man's lady friends. We had to send him home to explain to his wife why the car had been blown up and what it was all about. Unfortunately his car insurance doesn't cover a situation like this, so he won't be able to make a claim for the damage."

Police today advised anyone who comes across a suspect package to call officers to their home rather than risk danger moving the parcel.

REF 4

CLASSICAL ENVIRONMENTAL FOLLY

" "

REGISTERED AT STATIONS' HALL

EDITION 1   JULY 1991 PRE MAASTRICHT

EDITION 2 AUGUST 1991 CORRECTS EDITION 1

EDITION 3 SEPTEMBER 1991 CORRECTS EDITION 2

EDITION 4 NOVEMBER 1991 POST MAASTRICHT EDITION

EDITION 5 SEPTEMBER1992

EDITION ADDS TO CHAPTERS 5- 6- 7 and 9

Acknowledgments and thanks are given to many friends who encouraged the completion of this work during its long gestation period and to those who pointed out errors.

Daniel Tissington

i

INDEX

INDEX ----------------------------- PAGE i

PREFACE ----------------------------- PAGE ii

CHAPTER 1 LIMITS AND RATIONALE DEFINED PAGE 1

CHAPTER 2 OTHER ENVIRONMENTAL PROBLEMS PAGE 3

CHAPTER 3 COMMON SHORTFALL OF GOVERNMENTS PAGE 13

CHAPTER 4 CONSERVATION/PRESERVATION MISCONCEPTIONS [BIRDS AND ANIMALS] PAGE 22

CHAPTER 5 CONSERVATION/PRESERVATION MISCONCEPTIONS [PLANTS AND BUILDINGS] PAGE 27

CHAPTER 6 POSSIBLE SOLUTIONS TO OZONE LAYER DEPLETION AND ENHANCED GREENHOUSE EFFECT PAGE 38

CHAPTER 7 PLANNING ACTS PAGE 42

CHAPTER 8 WATER DISTRIBUTION PAGE 47

CHAPTER 9 DISCUSSION/CONCLUSIONS PAGE 52

CHAPTER 10 SOME RECOMMENDATIONS PAGE 56

ii

PREFACE

This work endeavours to set out and to consider matters concerning human survival, a matter which the Writer has termed ' societies problem '. It seems that excessive extraction of food for human consumption and fuel for power supplies from the Earth's crust and seas have not been given sufficient serious thought.....and the factors governing this plunder are being ignored almost world wide for one reason or another. Resultant pollution is not being properly dealt with....or more to the point, some of it cannot be dealt with... or so it seems.

There appears to be two overriding causes of Societies Problem, ie

[1A] humanity fulfilling nature's requirement and
[2B] political shortcomings.

These points are expanded as follows

1A] Population growth, which seems to be caused by Natures subtle programming of all living species; including humans.
2B] Most governments are facilitating the plunder of Mother Earth by imposing excessive tax levels coupled with unnecessary and ill founded legislation thereby separately enhancing suitable conditions for population growth as in 1A above.

The Reader's indulgence is requested whilst the scene is set to enable analysis, solutions and conclusions to be set out.

It matters not how long it takes to achieve political reform on the lines set out in this work, or indeed, any other changes that are thought to be needed. What matters is that modification is still possible. Political union with the Common Market will probably make change as impossible as it used to be in the USSR....because of the hoards of bureaucratic civil servants that will reign supreme within its structure!

CHAPTER 1 1.

LIMITS AND RATIONALE DEFINED

Perhaps the best way to reach out to minds that may be
blinded by need, tradition, camouflage, conditioning
...not forgetting featherbedding is to ask why humanity
is here and what life is all about. This question
immediately raises the problem of religious beliefs.
However long held tradition advises against the mixing
of religion and politics, even Christ said 'give unto
Caesar', so this work will pass this important side of
matters to the theologian.

The responsibility for feeding a young family in the
'70s served to heighten the unease felt by the Writer
because of the famines that reccured from time to time
in India and, in the '60s, Biafra. Inability to utilise
part of the rear of a quarter acre garden as vegetable
plot, in order to give some insurance against ever
having to tell my children that there is no food,
because of faulty environmental laws added puzzlement to
my apprehension. Whereas the UK environmental
legislation then in existence may have served well if it
had been enforced in a different manner rather than as
various officials who were able to control events used
their powers, then this work may never have been been
thought necessary. Although responsibility for the
children is now at an end, organically produced
vegetables are grown as a healthy retirement hobby for
the Writer and his Wife's consumption.

It maybe this is the place to point out that Mother
Nature has minimum requirements if mankind is to survive
as a species but major deviations from these
requirements brought about to serve whims or incorrect
beliefs have to be paid for in full. Since many of the
officers and elected bodies of the world's various
political systems liaise with each other much of the
world's legislation is, as far as can be seen, similar.
In any event, the price that Mother Nature demands to

2

enable mankind to escape the fate of the dinosaur applies universally and it is thought that the general line of the philosophy given in the following text is applicable worldwide.

If then a wide view point is taken in an attempt to answer the question poised ' why is humanity here and what is life all about ' then it maybe best answered by observing the behavioural patterns of other forms of life that surround us and watch for parallels in human behaviour. In so doing, the Writer eventually reached a number of conclusions....but let us examine these matters together in a logical manner, declare conclusions, look at what is required in light of findings and offer solutions. In this way, we can compare what political and social guidelines should be about with what they appear to be about. The shortfall can then be shown in view of requirement.

CHAPTER 2

3

OTHER ENVIRONMENTAL PROBLEMS

Let us look at the enjoyable and healthy pursuit of gardening. Whether we are interested in production of flowers, vegetables or even a modicum of either, requirement for a well drained, nourished soil is paramount. Experts talk of the need for compost to provide some of these and other essential requirements. As a result, many of us possess a compost heap.

The compost heap consists of discarded vegetable matter which is required to ' rot down '. Generally, this process of 'rotting' can occur in a 'heap' without aid from the gardener. However, the 'rotting ' process can be accelerated by suitable chemical additives which maybe bought from garden seed merchants and similar specialists. Various agents may be added by the manufacturer of the preparation to enable the rotting process to get a good start. Alternatively, the gardener may decide to speed the process by the simple addition of animal or bird excreta.

Such a compost heap now forms a simple environment for a host of unrelated micro organisms. Assuming conditions of this provided environment are suitable, that is the make up of the heap is moist enough, the temperature and pH is within the required range and the texture of the heap is suitably tender, the build up of numbers of these microscopic forms of life is very rapid indeed. [Hard woody materials will compost over a period but are best dried and burnt to provide pot-ash and prevent disease.] The physical activity and chemical output of these minuscule creatures can, under ideal conditions, produce very high temperatures. Indeed, many a hayrick has been burnt down by spontaneous combustion caused by similar action. However, the normal compost heap which usually reaches high temperatures rarely, if ever, catches fire. The heap will, however, eventually become exhausted of nutrients and most of the little creatures

4

who reside therein will die of starvation. That is, the compost heap's form of Government, which may be Mother Nature didn't, or couldn't, foresee and safeguard the future....or maybe the programme for these tiny creatures was purpose set to provide plant support and their survival is of no importance.

Similar phenomenon can be observed with the aid of suitable apparatus by the brewers of alcoholic drinks such as wine and beer. The environment put together by the brewer consists principally of water and sugar although malt or ginger flavouring is often added to beer. Malt, made from barley, also produces a suitable surface tension to the fluid in order to maintain a frothy head for a greater period of time in the finished product. Ginger or malt additives do not adversely affect the simple organism, namely yeast, which is introduced by the brewer in order that alcohol is produced. Unlike the compost heap, these alcoholic fluids or potential drinks are produced under sterile conditions and great care is taken to keep the yeast strain pure and to keep other living organisms out of the prepared solution. These simple yeast cells will, assuming the environment is held at a suitable pH and temperature, multiply by division. Each division will produce roughly equal parts of alcohol and CO_2 gas.

Steps must be taken by the brewer to maintain these alcoholic fluids at an acceptable state in order to encourage large numbers of yeast cell divisions to take place. Care must also be taken to keep the fluid under a blanket of CO_2 lest the oxygen content of the human environment oxidizes the fluid. Beer or wine that has been exposed in this way becomes oxidized and tainted. It therefore becomes unpleasant to drink.

When undergoing fermentation, yeast cells, which are kept disease and predator free, prosper and multiply in their billions .....until all of the sugar is consumed or until the alcoholic content of their environment reaches 10% to 15%. The exact percentage level at which the Yeast's environment inhibits further division, when

5

alcohol production ceases, depends upon the type or
strain of yeast employed. It matters not. The yeast
will eventually poison its environment or exhaust its
food resources and its activities are then suspended.

Let us briefly look at another, and unrelated species,
that is, the sockeye salmon. This fish starts its life
cycle as an egg upstream in a reasonably pollution free
river. It is obvious that such a river need not consist
of the purist distilled water....since rivers were
originally natural land drains which carried excesses
of water, mixed with sewage of man and beast, to the
sea. The fledgling salmon start their lengthy and
perilous journey in which the fittest, wariest and
luckiest young fish elude predators and reach the sea.
In the oceans of the world these growing fish migrate
some considerable distance involving thousands of miles
over a period of time, and then return to the river of
their origin in prime condition in order to spawn....and
   immediately die.

Each of these forms of life, and there are many other
suitable examples we could examine, briefly looked at
in the last few paragraphs are clearly programmed to
perform nature's requirement, that is to reproduce their
kind in great numbers. As such, the smaller and simpler
species appear to have little 'free choice' over the
actions carried out in their brief existences. Higher
forms of life, such as the salmon, are, it seems,
similarly programmed, but appear to have a much greater
degree of freedom over their closely regulated lives.
For example, they appear to be able to choose to go to
the left, right or straight ahead to collect food or
avoid a predator.....or so it seems. But the overriding
part of each programme, which appears common to all the
species is procreation of its own kind. This compelling
programme appears to extend its powerful influence to
all earthbound species. It is so strong and inescapable
that adequate numbers are produced by each species to
ensure continuity of their kind in the face of the
requirements of the foodchain, disease, famine, war or
what have you.

6

It may have occured to the Reader that in certain spheres man achieves somewhat similar results to other less aware forms of life that share this planet Earth with him. Admittedly, we humans seem to have a much greater degree of freedom over our lives than ' the other species '. However, the puzzling fact remains... that in many of our activities we seem to produce a very similar result to that of, for example, yeast. For a start, look at the human problems associated with the Horn of Africa. There, the procreation of human beings has outstripped the resources [rain and therefore food crops] of the area. Those who send food to such areas should understand the predicaments that they will cause if, as is natural, these unfortunates, once fed, go forth and multiply their kind. Admittedly, these dreadful effects are magnified in some parts by war. But mankind in general does not readily associate the problems of the Horn with his own comparatively cosy little part of the world. After all, the shelves of the super markets are full and we all know about the huge and costly reserves of the Common Market's food mountain. However, one year's world wide disaster with the production of arable crops from the effects of weather, from the enhanced greenhouse effect, a nuclear winter, migratory insects or disease and the food mountain would be reduced to nil overnight...assuming one could still find the means to transport and refrigerate the stored victuals. Yes, I can hear the Reader say, but this sort of outlook is melodramatic...but is it? Locusts were recently [1988] reported in large numbers in the USA. Speculation had it that the insects had flown the Atlantic aided by a prevailing wind. In 1988 and 1989, severe drought also plagued the corn producing belts of North America. Farmers there experienced crop failure on a massive scale. But do I hear the cynic say ' are we not still eating ?' If my ears did not deceive me, one still has to concede that the mechanism for disaster is present and perhaps we should remind ourselves of the famine caused by a decade or so of incessant rain which killed millions of Europeans in the Middle Ages...or the more

7

recent Irish potato famine. To make matters infinitely worse the human population is still growing worldwide. Whereas most can easily foresee the consequential unemployment of a factory workforce, for example, that loses or completes a large contract...fewer seem to be able to 'see' the future for expanding human numbers when food production or energy requirements cannot keep pace with needs.

Undoubtedly, the world's expanding human population is occurring under the influence of a subtle programme instilled by nature in which it appears to offer its 'subjects' a free choice. But more about that aspect of things later. For now, let us return to the salmon. It may provide a low key insight to the examination of the problem in hand. Such an approach is desirable since the Writer, in his youth, rejected outright claims that human beings were programmed because the matter was not portrayed in a delicate and plausible manner.

The young salmon, when it sees an inedible moving object veers away. This avoiding action is swift and sometimes indicative of panic when the object is large and appears to threaten the fish. In other words, the salmon generally proceeds down river, upriver or along its migratory ocean track deviating slightly here and there to take food or avoid danger. The salmon, if it thinks at all, may well believe it carries out these manoeuvres on an entirely voluntary basis. However, the observer recognises the likelihood that its acts are governed by an inner mechanism which may equate to a man's feeling of pleasure, fear, hunger pangs etc; since the untutored salmon can hardly be expected to know it or its kind will become extinct, starve to death or provide a predator with a meal if it fails to carry out specific functions. That is, the fish is subtly programmed. It seems to the Writer that the human species is also programmed but may also be granted an unspecified degree of freedom of choice. The question of how much freedom of choice a human has got is difficult to answer, particularly since the degree of freedom enjoyed appears to vary with age and with the

8

individual. None the less, an attempt to 'provide a glimpse' of this unknown will be made.

Let us consider a ripe, rosy eating apple overhanging a garden fence and within sight and reach of people walking along the pavement. Let us assume that each of the passing pedestrians that enjoy eating apples will observe this succulent fruit. Most, if the apple is within easy reach, will contemplate picking it. Many of the more elderly observers will inhibit the temptations in case someone is watching whilst others will sternly chastise themselves as they dismiss the temptation to commit a felony.....unless, that is, they haven't eaten for a few days.

None the less, to quite a few of the younger observers of this temptation, scrumping will be a thrilling hobby. Therefore some will look up and down the road and take a chance if the way to do so appears clear. However, if a few policeman are in varying nearby positions, only some of the starving observers or the cheekiest of urchins will still take a chance and pluck the apple.

It must be remembered that the human brain is the subject of much investigation and is still not properly understood. One of the many puzzles the brain poses is that since all the biological sensors produce and transmit similar electrical signals to the brain, how do we differentiate between, for example, sound and sight.....particularly since there is no one inside the head to 'see these decoded physiological experiences ' so to speak. However, from the foregoing and other similar examples of human behaviour, we can form a model which may, or may not be, factual but which should enable each of us to reach an insight of our suspected programming and its limits.

It would seem to the Writer that we human beings can over-ride nature's requirements when aided by fear of consequence or pangs of conscience. The degree of conscience exercised by an individual is probably related to disciplinary measures experienced during

9

one's upbringing and maybe largely ingrained at that time by feelings of respect and especially 'fear of the consequences'. The supposition in no way clashes with the old adage 'spare the rod and spoil the child'. And to counter possible reaction which may take the line that 'the thoughts of the ancients' are out of date it might be a good opportunity to point out that human beings have not significantly altered over the centuries. Due to the ability to read and write knowledge has become additive. But it seems our basic behavioural patterns,

[a] birth and storage of genes during development,
[b] passing on our genes to future generations,
[c] caring for off spring,
[d] fading away,
occur over and over down the passages of time somewhat like a gramophone record played over and over. Furtherto, our daily activities, which we carry out naturally, such as working, eating and sleeping appear to be something we wish to do and yet may merely be a form of programmed support to enable the main requirement to be carried out. However, to over-ride a requirement or temptation of nature is not all that easy; but can be partially successful when need is coupled with conscious effort.

As already shown, the effects of overpopulation in yeast bring about pollution of the tiny organism's environment. Over population of the human sphere achieves a similar effect. It must be clear to all that household rubbish from the civilized parts of the world reaches enormous volumes. Indeed, Local Authorities, whose responsibility it is to dispose of these mountains of refuse, have difficulty in finding suitable places in which to tip the waste. Additionally, when such sites are found, the land is unsafe for some other purposes for long periods of time because of gases that are generated from the deposited cast-offs. Sewage is another pollution which creates serious problems with the purity of rivers and oceans alike.... but only when produced by excessive numbers of densely located people

10

or other large animals.

Other serious but less publicized forms of pollution are
produced to satisfy the needs of excessive numbers of
humans. For example, the production of pork, poultry,
beef and lamb for human food may add to the raw sewage
introduced to the rivers and oceans of the world. This
type of pollution is potentially more serious in some
ways since very little of it is treated in sewage farms.
And then there is serious pollution from spilled fluids
produced in the manufacture of cattle food, namely
silage. Indeed, the destruction of the S American rain
forests, and its part in the enhanced greenhouse effect,
is partly fuelled by the enormous beef requirement of
hungry humans world wide.

To the foregoing, we must include large areas of
concrete. There is concrete for houses, garages,
driveways, highways, runways, motor ways, public car
parks, private car parks, pavements, factories, hotels,
railways, government offices and farmyards. We must not
forget the pollution from fuel, including nuclear waste,
utilised or burnt to provide heat, lighting,
household/factory requirements, transport and freight
movement; all of which is required to support the huge
numbers of people that hunger to be served with the
needs of life. And lest we forget, there is the
'greenhouse' effect which is accelerating toward the
danger level. This effect is brought about by gases,
some of which are formed by the burning or utilising of
fossil fuel. Finally, there is the pollution generated
and dispersed in the manufacture and use of pesticides
and herbicides, fungicides and fertiliser. These poisons
are required to produces the necessary high yields of
foodstuff per acre on an economic basis.....which some
claim [probably correctly] cause polluted food and
nitrate saturated drinking water. It maybe that these
effects are more readily noticed in densely packed
nations such as GB...but the population levels of places
with space to spare, such as Canada, are noticeably
expanding...as are nations without space to spare such
as India and China.

11

Whereas it is often quoted that the World's entire population could be accomodated in the standing position on the Isle of Wight, there is no possibility of each individual's support requirements being included in this tiny area.

At this point, one may begin to wonder about the actual acreage demanded to satisfy each head of the population of Europe, USSR, USA, and the potential requirements of the huge populations of India, China, Africa and S America. People the world over need shelter, the means to produce and pay for food to eat, the means to earn a living and reproduce themselves.... ie SPACE. In the past, the occupants of GB and other developed Countries have deforested the land to provide the required resources. Others, who follow this example are now criticized for destroying the environment required to sustain our chosen way of life. Clearly some of us in the developed parts of the World have taken more out of Mother Earth than 'our share'. And, if the beliefs set out earlier that Humans do have the freedom to over-ride ' their programme ' limiting, or reducing population growth henceforth may, nay, should surely be the number one priority in ALL parts of the World.

One perhaps begins to think of the huge problems thus presented to the HUMAN RACE. Such thoughts begin to put into perspective the shallow bleatings, but in many cases sincerely held beliefs, made about the declining wildlife populations*, the destruction of the rain forests and the building of houses/factories or hospitals on green field sites. That is, the originators of 'the bleatings' appear to be trying to cure the individual parts of societies problem that annoys or affects them whilst ignoring the basic cause of the malady. One also starts to wonder why the various expensive and overmanned national and local government departments are not offering guidance to the government or the public in these matters. Indeed, successive governments, almost certainly with the blessing of their officals, actually pay the public to produce off spring

12

by means of family allowances. No wonder the newspapers report the existence of various superdads. One then begins to suspect that successive governments have drifted into, or perhaps been led into, the role of bee keeper ...ie the public appear to be farmed. There maybe reasons for this suspected trend which we will explore in due course.

*It is acknowledged that declining populations of elephant and other ivory producing species are subjected to additional forms of pressure from the ivory poacher's gun. Other species maybe under threat for their pelts or to act as trophies.

CHAPTER 3   13

COMMON SHORTFALL OF GOVERNMENTS

No one with real understanding of life would advocate the banishment of government who generate the law for their countrymen. Indeed, without law there would be no order or ownership at all. Strong arm thugs would soon discover it is easier to evict the old and weak from their houses, for example, than to pay off 'a mortgage'. However, this philosophy should not be considered as an 'invite' to go down the road of going soft on the old... as officialdom sometimes seem inclined to do...a concession which some old folk appear quick to take unfair advantage of. Never the less, it is not desirable that government should seek to regulate every facet of the population's affairs. This suggestion appears to be recognised by some administrations. Indeed, great strides have been made in UK and Europe to reduce the role of 'Nanny Government' during recent times. But the fact remains that UK national and local government do still wield far too much power over the British Public. Furthermore, in 1990, some sources claim that the UK authorities now deploy about 40% of the nation's income...a recent fall from around a maximum of about 47%. The Writer thinks that if one takes account of successive taxation levied on many UK goods the actual figure might be much higher than 40%! The same source claims that governments of some other industrialised nations dispose of an even greater proportion of their national income. However, some of this seemingly excessive expenditure maybe justified whilst a nation's defence needs are paramount and or national debt is being repaid. Nevertheless, excessive population levels, generally speaking, make the call for large numbers of bureaucratic government employees and the consequential expenditure and waste appear excusable. Indeed, many of the bureaucrats which man these establishments, and we cannot exclude the 'many extra millions' potentially hovering over the European Community, are avidly

14

seeking to obtain more influence, more power, bigger budgets, more staff, bigger salaries and bigger inflation proofed pensions. And because bureaucrats are not subjected to the rigours of election, they can enjoy the benefits of 'long term' political steerage. As such, over a prolonged period, almost any of their aims maybe achievable without arousing the suspicions of a casual observer. It maybe that this reasoning goes part way in explaining why polititicans do not seem to be able to exercise adequate control over their civil servants. Whereas ambition is a normal human trait most of us have to curtail our desires for reasons of economics. In ministerial and government circles, the limits are much less restricted, for taxes are extracted under threat of penalty...which can include incarceration of any defaulter. In such circumstances, demands should be restrained...rather than extracting that which 'can be got away with'....often to be wasted because of the precedent set by neighbouring nations. The US President, Mr Bush, has shown recognition of the economic effects that laying off two million civil servants would have on US 1990 budget deficit, but even he may have missed the serious environmental point at issue which this work will endevour to set out. Further, but limited, economic understanding has been shown in the UK for it is now recognised that central government should not control or finance State Corporations on taxpayers money. As such, some privatisation schemes have already been completed, and more are scheduled for the near future. However, some UK Local Authorities still seem to continue the practice of running businesses [sometimes under the guise as local amenities]. It is not considered an acceptable excuse to say such policies save the taxpayer money WHEN a profit is made since any business ventures can fail. And yet it seems that in many cases local taxes are set as high as can be 'got away with' regardless. Let us draw attention to other expensive habits which are 'on the local community and

15

which cannot really be justified even if they are not abused. 'Town Twinning' is one such activity and providing single parents with privileged accomodation [and rent and furniture on Social Security] appears to be another. Some young women, it is said, deliberately get pregnant to obtain their 'own accomodation' And then one reads of councillors who draw excessive expenses. Further economic measures to control the UK economy include raising interest levels....a method which achieves the necessary results but appears unbalanced in as much as civil servants manning levels and government expenditure is not reduced in proper proportion. When government cuts are made, they usually apply to services only. Therefore, the numbers of civil servants/amount of government expenditure [local or national] never begins to approach a proper and balanced level.

There is nothing benevolent about 'spending or wasting another's money'......and the point can be clearly made if it is imagined what would happen if the ordinary taxpayer had a legalised right to an unspecified chunk of the contents of a bank account belonging to a councillor or an elected member of a national government. The point maybe brought home even clearer if one realises that for every aged victim of hyperthermia, thousands shiver their way through cold winters. And whereas tears should not be shed on sufferers who have frittered earnings on expensive holidays or who have indulged in other frivolous lavishness before providing for retirement, perhaps such facts ought to make wasteful extraction of taxes a criminal act. Indeed, such extortion, which may amount to a sort of legalised Robin Hood act, may-be indistinguishable from demanding money with menaces.

For the foregoing reasons alone, and there maybe other reasons, ministerial costs, governmental budgets and local tax demands will not automatically reduce. Apart

16

from the undesirable BIG BROTHER aspects of 'Nanny Government' there are other serious considerations to be taken into account. Nature provided mankind with nerve ends to ensure that discomfort from unpleasant or harmful occurrences compel an individual to take steps to protect him or herself. Excessive feather bedding of healthy or undeserving individuals by 'protective legislation' anaesthetizes the nerve ends and causes decay in a nation's well being. For example, one hears of occurrences in the UK where people will watch a rape, a mugging or an act of criminal damage being committed and yet will not intervene or stand as witnesses because they don't want to become involved. It must be pointed out that silent witnesses destroy their own security by not ensuring justice is served. Such is the state in the U K that even if one feels compelled to intervene physically the law will sometimes side with the thug. Difficult as it maybe to bring about it is perhaps time for the delicate balance between admissible intervention and street brawls is reset....since unlike public figures, an ordinary member of the public is not usually given plain clothed or uniformed guard around the clock...or at all. This paragraph introduces some of the undesirable social effects that excessive government benevolence brings about.

The point is that excesses of any kind, however well intended, seem to lead to disaster. One has only to look at the Eastern Block and see what an army of bureaucrats and their unbalanced military spending has achieved to illustrate the point...a situation which even their isolated 'iron curtain' tactics couldn't remedy. But in order to obtain a sense of balanced consideration, let us look at a further build up of evidence to substantiate the claim in a more orderly manner.

The findings of anthropologists investigating Easter Island may form an instructive example. The Island is

17

thought to have been originally colonized by the Polynesians. As the reader will probably know, the Island is endowed with some six hundred enormous statues depicting human figures, some of which are 40 feet in height. These mysterious workings have been carved out of solid rock with primitive stone tools. Some of the work pieces, weighing up to 70 tons, have been painstakingly transported to various parts of the Island by, it is thought, the use of rollers and levers constructed from tree trunks.

Clearly, the Island's original industry which involved the production and siting of these ancient monuments needed a huge skilled stonemason and labouring workforce. The non-mechanised backup which surely must have included laborious tree felling on a massive scale... also involved the feeding and clothing of the entire labour pool and their families. Control and management of a field force deployed over such a widespread area must have presented problems requiring many public servants or bureaucrats because of the total lack of modern communications. It is not clear whether the operation was of a political or religious nature, or a mixture of both elements. But it matters little, the bureaucrats or high priests built and controlled what was obviously a thriving and successful community . But this form of social engineering did not endure. The production of statues ceased with many half completed models still attached to and entombed in massive chunks of rock face. The population level fell dramatically and the hustle and bustle of the once healthy community never recovered.

What happened to produce this savage decline in the population is a matter of opinion and speculation. However, one proffered version of events seems to turn on the excessive tree felling operations which resulted in soil erosion. The consequential crop failures meant

18

that the successful build up of population numbers could not be maintained in spite of apparent political, economic and social success. The weakened and defenceless colony was later plundered by slave traders, or so it is said. So much for the excesses of statue carving and tree felling.

The decline of the Roman Empire and Nazi Germany might well be attributed to excesses that each regime practiced. In any event, these particular histories tend to confirm the earlier suggestion that a link exists between National excesses and social decline.

If we now return to the world wide problems of today, and reconsider the claim that many political systems deploy almost half of their nation's income...it must be clear that the required tax level can only be met by increasing the cost of each product or by increased productivity. The justification of these results, in as far as they can be justified, appears to be that the cost increase is alright provided that competitive nations cost per unit are comparable. But this blinkered approach appears to neglect the environmental impact that such economic jiggery pokery helps to bring about. The added cost supports increased population levels and associated plunder of the earth's resourses....ie MORE POLLUTION of every kind! Just how much impact will the hoards of bureaucrats employed to administer the Common Market's proposed political union exert on the world in general.......and the UK in particular?

It maybe that at this stage, we should attempt to obtain a sobering base line. One may, perhaps, provide such a sense of proportion by pointing out that it is estimated by some experts that the sun consumes some thousands of tons of matter per second. It follows that at this rate of consumption, a rate which is thought to have been sustained for some five billion years, the sun

19

has a finite lifetime. When this ball of heat cools, the activities of the human race and its important institutions are doomed.....although it is perhaps possible that the genes of Homo Sapiens at least maybe transported to perpetuate his kind in other still friendly regions of space.

Let us again ask ' What then is life all about'? In view of the foregoing it would seem logical to make the best of the time we have. That is, a framework should be aimed at that allows all to work for their own required standard of living with meaningful penalties for upsetting the delicate balances of Mother Earth by collectively

a] taking more than Mother Earth can continually and safely supply.

b] creating excessive pollution

c] not having to toil for half, or more, of a working life in order to finance overmanned and, some say, overbearing Commonmarket, federal, ministry and town hall bureaucrats.

Such a programme would, ideally and logically, have to include a radical reduction in the levels of the human population. Alternatively, humans could easily end up living like unfortunate battery hens and squabbling like experimental rats in overcrowded laboratory cages. Worse still, these unfortunates would be short of conventional fuel or under threat of pollution from nuclear reactor waste....conditions which will affect the public and bureaucrats alike. The point becomes much clearer when one compares life as portrayed in the Bronx with life in a small market town or village. Added to the foregoing there would be a shortage of food. [Such a possibility makes a nonsense of the call of yesteryear

20

in which there was a cry from Europe to increase the birth rate to consume its 'food mountain'] The foregoing projections therefore seem a distinct possibility. More especially since nuclear waste, a by-product from nuclear generating systems utilising the fission process, [a process utilising a controlled rate of an atom bomb explosion] is currently produced at a rate which exceeds its own decay time. And there is a call in some quarters for more nuclear electrical generating stations which are considered essential to meet, we are told, foreseeable demand. If, we are told, a controlled fusion electricity generating process [a controlled hydrogen bomb explosion] could be successfully developed in engineering terms, cheap [methinks we have heard these claims before] and almost unlimited power with much reduced radioactive pollution would become available. However, this elusive benefit to mankind would not create space for building [and other essential human life support requirements] which is already restricted by countries operating repressive planning laws.* UK planning laws allow the Planners to create a scarcity of land available for residential development. [These procedures are probably justifiable if demand for housing continues to spiral] It follows, that to satisfy the laws of supply and demand, the cost of building land has, in places, reached hundreds of thousands of pounds per acre. In order to keep housing costs limited to a semi affordable level [limited by the need for competitive costs of goods produced for export] it becomes necessary to construct high rise flats since 'four to the acre' is claimed to represent too low a building density. As a result of all the foregoing reasoning, it is suggested worldwide population levels should, initially, for evaluation puposes be halved. Perhaps the matter should be reconsidered when the recommended population level is reached since it maybe that Mother Earth cannot safely and continously support even half the world's present population either!

21

It is obvious that if the central theme to this problem, ie the excessive and expanding worldwide population level, is sorted out by people themselves....and with modern birth control technology it is within the grasp of enlightened populations....that govenments must work, or be made to work, with the population to prepare for a task that will take many, many decades to achieve. Of course the bureaucrats will object to and advise against the scheme on the grounds that serious economic problems can be expected if populations are 'run down' to' sensible and affordable' levels. Such suggestions should be discounted and would, no doubt, be off set to a great extent by the possibility of drastic reductions in the levels of civil servants employed. Indeed, the lead nation in such an exercise could well experience an economic upturn as falling taxation drastically cut production costs. Of course, the matter of population reduction can be ignored. But Nature will eventually sort matters out, indeed, may have already started, if persistently provoked and probably in a most brutal, inconsiderate and unacceptable way.

Finally, it seems clear that the public need additional political safe guards....a mechanism which if already in place appears generally not to be working effectivly. Let us explore together more of the detail which suggests that successive governments have been led, and are, in turn, leading the public to a disastrous consequence.

*A recent discovery seems to indicate that vast reserves of solid methane nodules, an environmentally clean source of energy, exists below the World's Oceans. This beneficial facility, assuming severe mining problems can be overcome, will not alter the case for a reduction of worldwide population levels...since lack of space and excessive pollution levels would still pose a real hazard to humanities existence.

CHAPTER 4

·22

CONSERVATION/PRESERVATION MISCONCEPTIONS [BIRDS AND ANIMALS]

Some of the developed world's legislation, and in particular, Great Britian's, purports to safeguard 'The Nation's Heritage" in the form of Conservation or Preservation Orders, Countryside Acts and Listed Buildings. However, much of this legislation is thought to be somewhat misguided technically. In many cases, such Acts appear to be adopting Communist ideals in as much as they deny the basic meaning of ownership.

This contradiction to our way of life maybe in place for any one of a number of reasons....or for a variety of reasons. For example, it appears that successive UK Governments have tried to satisfy the requirements of concerned and often sentimental but misguided members of the public. It may even be that the public is being brainwashed by bureaucrats who may not know any better or perhaps know when they are onto a good thing. Observation would suggest that a similar situation applies to many civilised countries. It matters not who copied who...many wrongs do not alter the facts. Let us look at some points which tend to confirm what is suspected.

Provided the climate and available space is satisfactory for a given species of wild life, and a supply of suitable nutrient and water is available, adequate procreation to ensure continuity of a given species is almost guaranteed. For example, let us look at two of the most persecuted animals of all time....namely the rat and the rabbit. There is no sign of either species being made extinct in spite of man's best efforts. The above claims can be safely made even though traps, snares, dogs, ferrets, chemical and biological warfare has been unleashed without mercy on these unfortunate creatures. However, one has to admit that the rabbit population has been partially contained since the inhuman introduction of myxomatosis. But eventually, as always, Mother Nature will preserve 'the balance' by

23

producing a strain of rabbit immune to this particular disease.

One also has to take into account that the rabbit, prior to the introduction of myxomatosis, created large areas of desert in each and every corn field.... that is, the rabbit is a costly pest. The point in its favour is that the animal performed a useful function in helping to feed many pre-war Britons in what were difficult economic times pre World War 2.

Bats, it is claimed by those that study these mammals, are declining in numbers. These creatures are protected by law even though no one [as far as is known] hunts them in GB. Indeed, the only occurrence of persons 'persecuting' bats that the Writer is aware of, are alarmed householders who find their lofts invaded. And why not. Whose house is it you may well ask? These creatures are much like flying mice and it seems a bit much to expect people to harbour wild life of this or any other sort in their lofts against their own better judgement...or at the whim of some so called conservationist... as the law currently seems to demand. Such comment is even more valid, if, as one suspects, some of these creatures are infested with lice. 'Conservationists' may well say that the numbers of barns have reduced and therefore we need to allow the little creatures to roost where they can.

How then, we may then ask, did these flying mammals manage to survive before there were such things as 'Conservationists', barns and houses? After all, the number of caves originally available to bats for roosting purposes have not significantly decreased in numbers....and man ceased to live in them centuries ago. The possibility must be faced that IF there is a decline in numbers of UK Bats its more likely to be because there is insufficient suitable food available. Or it maybe that their food supply, which is composed largely of insects , is unsuitable or short in supply because it is adversely affected by pesticides.

24

The resilience of a species to recover depleted numbers is illustrated by the Magpie. This destructive bird [it ransacks other birds nests consuming their eggs and fledgelings] was only seen in ones and twos at half mile or so range in the Berkshire Countryside during the late thirties. Today, this species is protected and is seen in 'plague' proportions in most urban areas. The Bullfinch, another destructive bird, it completely strips fruit trees and bushes of fruit buds, is now much rarer than hitherto. However, the bird is not extinct in spite of harsh, but necessary, persecution.

It appears to the Writer that if a species enjoys adequate supplies of food and space it will find the ability to survive. One can look for further endorsement of this supposition in the way that wild cats, dogs, foxes, rats and mice are reported living wild in the suburbs. Admittedly, the larger species may have trouble finding adequate space to survive, particularly if humans exploit the subjects constituent parts for commercial gain or that the creatures own needs seriously encroach on human requirements.

From generalised observation, it must be clear that space requirements of wild life expands dramatically as the size of the animal under consideration increases. The space needed to ensure survival of really big animals is vast as shown by the plight of some African mammals who are exploited by poachers for both sport and ivory. However, there maybe ways of making a given area effectively larger than it really is. For instance, one economical way of achieving this seemingly impossible feat, and simultaneously reducing the impact of irresponsible butchers, might be to prohibit the use of mechanical vehicles or aircraft in National Parks for any reason whatever. This form of control might be made more effective still by banning automatic and large bore weapons. Further inroads maybe had by limiting the number of porters allowed to accompany a safari. Additionally, and more to the point, realistic reduction of the human population would make an actual increase in acreage available to all wildlife. However, selection of 'first line' measures to curb African wild life slaughter' is really a matter for the appropriate government. But in matters of 'conservation' some seem to think 'their ideas', many of which appear to the Writer to be narrow in scope, should be carried out and 'minor' matters of ownership are to be ignored. However, it is not thought civil law should allow a Citizen of any Country to roughly and inconsiderately trample on another's God given rights!

Adding to the problem of people taking strong measures to get their 'conservation' viewpoints adopted at all costs is the growing army of people who appear to want to tag or otherwise survey every bird or animal in sight with leg rings or fit every other mammal with a radio transmitter. One becomes bemused at these acts which maybe acceptable in strictly limited cases where a creature is in danger of becoming extinct for unknown reasons. By way of example we may quote the red squirrel whose numbers are in decline in GB. One really wonders at times how all the species that have survived for thousands and thousands of years managed to reach the twentieth century without the aid of these 'gadgets' and the gadget fitters. One such character particularly impressed me by saying that the transmitter he was fitting to a particular tiny animal was quite harmless and only weighed ten percent of the subject's body weight. The claim appears to ignore the stress caused to a wild creature by handling and which is made apparent by the rapid and violent heart action of the victim. This particular character's weight was estimated to be about twelve stones and it was thought that he would be well aware of a collar weighing some seventeen pounds [about ten percent of his body weight] if such a device were to be fitted round his particular neck!

Whilst on the subject of insensitivities, intensive food production is an obvious area for comment.....particularly egg production involving battery hens. However, the need for such methods maybe necessary to feed the worlds rapidly growing numbers of humans. None the less, insensitivity maybe inbred into

26

humans. For example, how can one justify the cramped cage of a solitary songbird who is not only imprisoned in a cage which almost prohibits the stretching of a wing, but inhibits flying and ensures a life sentence of solitary confinement! And whereas there maybe little room for sentimentality in the affairs of nature there is no room, in the Writer's book, for what appears to be unnecessary and thoughtless cruelty either.

CHAPTER 5

27

CONSERVATION/PRESERVATION MISCONCEPTIONS
[PLANTS/BUILDINGS]

Trees and other plants are also 'preserved' by law
enshrined in Conservation and Tree Preservation Orders.
[TPO's] Trees, which are an essential and beautiful form
of life, are unfortunately the object of more irrational
and emotional ' care ' than almost any other form of
life..apart from perhaps the sacred cow in starving
India. As such, trees are a difficult subject to write
about. However, the matter should not be neglected in
this work; more particularly since much of the World's
forest and woodland is now in very poor condition. That
is, the leaves generally lack lustre and trees do not
flourish. As such, trees are disease prone and
frequently represent little more than 'scrubby'
apologies for woodland.

Whereas there maybe more than one cause for this sad
and sorry state of 'our' trees and woodlands, let us
examine what is thought to be the major causes of this
tragic state of affairs.

The writer, who as a Research Company Employee,
submitted, in the '60s, an idea to protect fruit tree
blossom from frost damage and was subsequently requested
to evaluate the scheme. In the process of this, the
invaluable interest and collaboration of an elderly
fruit grower was acquired. The gentleman concerned,
owned two densely planted orchards and acted as
consultant to some two hundred other fruit growers.
Since his living was derived from fruit born of healthy
trees rather than enforcing misguided Acts which appear
to be based on emotion, the gentleman had to know what
he was talking about in order to prosper. These orchards
consisted of dwarf apple and pear trees, that is, the
trees did not exceed seven feet in height. Spacing
between the trees was four by six feet. The
owner/planter indicated to me that although he had made
the orchards productive and profitable, he would
hesitate before exceeding these densities. Today, higher
orchard densities maybe achievable with a Canadian

28

variety of apple tree known as Ballerina but pesticide/fungicide spraying requirements would probably be grossly high, a factor which may well result in greater water pollution levels. However, my collaborator's chief concern was that the branches of the fruit trees should not entwine. It was pointed out to me that the shelter from wind provided by the closely planted trees made the orchard a haven for insect life....some of which attacked the blossom/fruit. Entanglement of the branches made matters worse and in order to prevent such occurrences, the trees were pruned on an almost non stop sequential basis. This frequent pruning activity was backed by almost daily spraying of foliage feed or protective sprays throughout the summer months.

A little thought and arithmetic will reveal that the planted density of these orchard trees was in excess of eighteen hundred trees per acre. When one looks at the deciduous woodlands of the UK and of many other countries and observes trees which can reach eighty or more feet in height, 'growing' at a similar density to the miniature orchard trees previously described, one can be sure something is amiss somewhere. Furthermore, and to their disadvantage, many forests are rarely thinned, often for reasons based on government regulations and so called conservation. Matters are frequently made worse by government officials who control public money, tree preservation and like orders and who are responsible for forest tree saplings which are grown, or even planted, a few feet apart. And one often sees grown 'environmentalists' encouraging children to plant oaks and other forest trees a few feet one from another. Even the Royal Parks at Windsor, England appear to be replanted in this damaging manner these days. Such actions make one despair since such antics can cause even more environmental trouble as the Writer knows from bitter experience. It took about eight years of almost continuous correspondance with a Local Authority, MPS and the Department of Environment in order to obtain relaxation of a TPO which permitted neighbouring trees to devastate the Writer's garden with

29

a multitude of fungus...a calamity which is mirrored in the following text. Although this particular garden was eventually restored to health, the legislation which gives officialdom the power to create such havoc, if they so wish, has not been rescinded.

To make matters much worse, forest trees are not generally sprayed in the UK. This latter omission is perhaps desirable from the public point of view since forest spraying in the USA has been reported as a human health hazard which is thought to have caused infant deformities/mortalities.

But one has to appreciate that the foliage of many of these individual forest trees, would, given the freedom, spread a canopy over a diameter of some fifty feet....or more. Therefore proper utilisation of land makes it impossible to support a healthy deciduous forest, of say mature oaks, for example, at a planned density greater than sixteen to the acre. Of course, a well managed forest would in practice contain perhaps two or three mature forest trees per acre as well as a slightly larger number of strategically spaced semi mature trees, established young trees, saplings and seedlings. Ideally, the trees at all stages, including mature trees, would be felled in a orderly way to provide a succession of trees through a healthy living forest....since one should not attempt to preserve trees and other living examples of Nature's creations which are primarily intended to be replaced by renewal. In various areas throughout such a forest an acre or so would be cleared here and there from time to time to allow seeds to sprout and take root. Tree seedlings, which occur naturally in clearings, can congregate in great numbers. Of consequence, their casualty rate, which may be due to grazing animals, trampling or unsuitable conditions, is very high indeed. The result is that the saplings that eventually win through are healthy. They also have better gale resistant characteristics than planted and staked saplings which do not have to forge a root system in hard, unprepared and bramble strewn ground in order to feed and remain

30

upright.

In nature's untamed expanses, its animal and plant species successfully fight out survival battles on a 'live or perish' basis. This 'cut and thrust' scheme works well until the species are faced with excessive human intervention with bulldozers, automatic weapons and chain saws which are utilised to satisfy human hunger for expansion or space due to excessively large human population's needs. Clearly, it can be seen that when other species have to compete with man's requirement for space and man's excellent machines, which are sometimes misused, the balance becomes upset and many of Nature's species cannot cope. The destruction of the South American Rain Forests provide an excellent example! Here we see the natural rain forests being decimated by chainsaw operators to enable the otherwise unemployed workforce to exist and cattle ranchers to satisfy the requirements of some of the fast food Hamburger Trade,....which in turn is necessitated to feed excessive numbers of city dwelling human beings.

One can obtain a better understanding of the actions of these chainsaw operators, some of whom may well know about the potential environmental damage their actions could bring about, by looking at the actions of recent UK rail strike victims who in their millions went to work in their cars to enable the mortgage repayments or whatever......in spite of the known consequences of the enhanced green house effect.

Much talk, which maybe exaggerated, is generated about ancient woodlands and the unique ability of trees to prevent soil erosion, generate oxygen and to 'breath water vapour'* into the air.[* Note the water vapour deposited on a sheet of glass laid on a lawn during a dry sunny day.......grass is just about as shallow rooted as any plant can be.] Whereas it is admitted that PROPERLY MANAGED trees are excellent at these attributed benefits to mankind, other forms of vegetation achieve a similar, if less dramatic, result......without incurring the damaging and expensive

31

side effects that badly or unmanaged trees are prone to
invoke. Generally speaking, excessively large emissions
of water vapour are not necessary except in rare
circumstances like that of the Panama Canal whose locks
are completely 'powered' by enormous amounts of
collected rain water. One should not overlook the insect
and disease ridden area the initial conditions exhibited
to the builders of this remarkable water way. This
environment, which defeated the French and gave the
successful American Engineers a good run for their
money, is typical of overcrowded woodland which is
tempered by elevated temperatures. Additionally,
insecticide 'smoke guns' can be seen in large numbers in
timbered portions of Canada near populated areas. The
insect population is dense and attack humans in spite of
the precautions taken. The Writer experienced similar
insect infestations which occured in the arctic north of
the Canadian mainland. However, associated disease was
not a problem in either area...probably because of the
cooler climate existing in these parts of the world. Of
course, in the general mayhem surrounding the subject
concerning environmental matters, one can easily
overlook the considerable amounts of rain that is
attributable to evaporation of ocean water.

And as for "ancient" woodland. The Writer can tell of
woodland containing near mature deciduous trees, orchids
and much of the makeup attributed to ancient Woodland.
This 'selfset' woodland evolved in a disused
Hertfordshire clay brick pit some fifty years ago. The
woodland, which is excellently managed by a retired
Estate Bailiff, Mr J R Harmston, has been known to the
Writer since the late 1960's.

Many people are aware of the immense and expensive
damage trees can cause to buildings and associated
drainage systems......which is unacceptable. However,
other, and lesser known problems occur in the
management, or mismanagement, of forestland. These
problems stem from fungus which thrives, and achieves
epidemic status, in wind sheltered, damp and sunstarved
conditions. Many of the overcrowded woodlands of GB [and

32

many overseas forests] meet the above requirement to a tee and as a result, fungus growth easily reach plague proportions....particularly in areas consisting of heavy, poorly drained and low land soils. As already pointed out, any of nature's species which enjoy ideal conditions without persecution spread their kind in dangerous abundance. [Look at Humanity's achievments for example.] Fungus, depending on the type, fulfils its destiny by one or other of two means. That is either from the production of spores which are freely distributed in vast quantities per minute from ripe underside gills or by subterranean fibre type rhizomes; some possessing extremely long range underground capabilities. Each mode of propagation will seek suitable and fertile conditions before identical recreation of the parent commences. Damp wood, especially damp dead and rotting wood, is an ideal medium on which to germinate fungus spores. Most woodland is sufficently neglected [dead and pruned wood should be burnt or shredded and returned to the soil whilst tree stumps should be removed from the soil...or treated] to ensure a plentiful area of unhealthy and unbalanced habitat. As such, the air, and to a lesser extent, the ground itself some distance from a neglected forest can be saturated with fungus spores and rhizomes.

Where the land surrounding unmanaged forest is heavy or low laying, poorly drained and/or sunstarved from sunblock, any form of horticulture is often nothing short of heartbreak. Aggressive fungus, particularly a variety found in the more temperate zones and known as Armillaria or Honey Fungus, will, at times, attack and kill trees, fruit trees or indeed practically any form of plant life. Where conditions are really favourable, the foregoing afflictions maybe added to by other varieties of fungus such as mildew, club root, silver leaf etc. In addition, such sheltered land becomes infested with insect life.... some of which carry and therefore help to distribute fungus spores. In order to prevent wilful or indifferent devastation of this kind to third parties land by those who 'defend their right' to do as they please on their land, or who are just plain indifferent to the plight of others...or who are just nasty, a minimum 'sunlight entitlement' should be enacted for each plot of land where sunblock is caused by shade from trees.* After all, one is not advocating that anyone should be prevented from keeping or cultivating a 'rain forest' provided they own a Continent on which to accomodate it. What is being suggested here is that no one should be allowed to steal anothers sunlight by misplaced trees to a degree which diseases or otherwise prevents proper, normal and even essential use of neighbouring land. It is therefore thought that power should be granted, through the Courts, to owners/users of land to enable a no nonsense claim to a minimum amount of sunlight where this is obstructed by trees. The Writer can well remember the attitude of one unsympathetic observer regarding the damage due to sunblock inflicted on his Hertfordshire garden. The Gentleman asked how our forefathers in earlier times managed to grow vegetables. It was pointed out to the questioner that in Feudal times the Lord of the Manor imposed a tithe in return for use of land, and would not allow such conditions to occur since it diminished his own income. It is relevant to point out that the lost safeguard has never been addressed by UK Government even after the Writer's ten year protest to many M P's. It is recorded that long term experiments forced on the Writer by local and ministerial bureaucrats enforcing a TPO showed that seven hours of sunlight in June [cloud permitting] is below the limit at which healthy and successful horticulture can be carried out at this latitude ... particularly on heavy land. [Although the number of hours sunlight available per year is identical worldwide, the quality and seasonal distribution factors vary considerably] At any rate, nine hours appears to be the minimum amount of sunlight [cloud permitting] which permits reasonable horticulture results on most types of soil in the temperate zones.

One such species of Fungi which utilises insect dispersal for propagation, and which many readers will remember, is Dutch Elm Disease. The epidemic of this

34

particular disease practically laid low the common elm in many countries in the sixties...and when one considers the forgoing paragraphs, it becomes clear that it is highly probable that this particular 'epidemic' of Dutch Elm was caused by mismanaged forests [partly by courtesy of Conservation Orders and Tree Preservation Orders] and, assisted in many cases, by misguided actions of some members of the public, some local government officals /councillors and some Department of Environment Inspectors. It was the findings of a Department of Environment Inspector regarding the trees that were damaging the Writer's garden that first alerted one to the apparent futility of Appeals/Inquiries. The opinion has since been reinforced in matters not concerned with trees.

Matters do not end here either. Wheat, oats and barley are now grown in such close order [necessary in order to obtain high yields] that they too suffer all sorts of related disorders from causes similar to those outlined for overcrowded woodland. As the reader may know, the seed of these plants is treated with anti fungi preparations prior to planting. Frequently, mercury compounds are employed to satisfy these requirements. The seedlings, and more mature plants are also sprayed from time to time with more necessary, but equally obnoxious, chemicals. One cannot be surprised when one is subsequently informed that most wholemeal bread is tainted with unspecified chemicals. Nor can one be quite sure that the fungus infections of the corn fields are not made worse from the masses of wind and insect borne spores generated by neglected or 'preserved' woodlands!

The repeated claims that damage to forest trees is caused by acid rain may be exaggerated, or even false. Consider an active volcano. It will spew out tons of molten lava...and the sulphur content of such outpourings is often very high indeed. Water from springs in the vicinity of such activity is almost always high in sulphurous content. But this acidic contamination appears not to prevent the growth of nearby trees. An example which stands out in the

35

Writer's memory, and since it is well known, will, perhaps, persuade the Reader of the validity of the point, is Sulphur Mountain at Banff, in the Canadian Rockies. Further evidence supporting the claim can be seen in the West Indies in general and St Lucia in particular. The Writer has also seen apple trees 'thrive' and produce in abundance in the UK although virtually unattended year after year on land made so alkaline by free range chickens that grass refused to grow. Recorded observations would suggest that trees are fairly tolerant of a wide range of pH values. Claims made in Hertfordshire and Dorset that trees were being adversely affected by car exhaust fumes do not ring true when one looks at the health of London's mature specimen road-side trees. It seems reasonable to suggest that proper care of forests should take precedent over expensive extraction of Sulphur derivatives emitted from coal burning power stations. After all, one couldn't raise a row of radishes without thinning to provide adequate growing room. To drive home the point about environmental claims that seem unfounded, reference is made to another 'scare' that keeps rearing its head and which maybe without substance. That is the use of lead pipes for domestic water supplies. As the Writer has pointed out elsewhere the Romans utilised lead pipes at Bath, UK and some of these these pipes have carried water non stop for best part of two thousand years. If this water took up lead in any significant quantity, or at all, there would be nothing left of the lead pipes after all this time. Of course, some local waters will contain different salts or chemical compounds which may take on tiny amounts of lead... but the Writer has never seen eroded lead water pipes. It must also be remembered that millions of the Writer's generation have survived, in 'good nick', to this day in spite of the almost exclusive use of lead water pipes and lead paint during their formative years. Indeed, the Writer applied lead paint on the exterior of his Hertfordshire Residence for nearly a quarter of a century and until 1986 without obvious ill effects...and has since introduced lead paint to his present abode in Dorset. So where and why do these persistent, expensive and

36

possibly misleading ideals such as banning of use of lead paint and replacing of existing water pipes spring from we may wonder? [admittedly in those far off days it was common practice to run off a gallon of water first thing in the morning before filling a kettle to make tea.] However, it is thought, one cannot claim the same acceptance for leaded petrol or mecury based tooth fillings!

Fir trees, which are frequently grown commercially, are not entirely excluded from the forgoing since these trees are also prone to the ravages of fungus..or though to a lesser extent than deciduous trees. The reason for their partial immunity is thought to be due in part to the natural oils contained in their sap line and in their cellular make up.

Wild flowers are another of the causes taken up by conservationists and which are, in many cases needlessly 'protected'. Admittedly, there is a shortage of some plants....but some of these are thought to be due to chemicals such as pesticides rather than due to children picking them. Let's face it, picking bluebells and cowslips is, or was, a time honoured event for country folk. And for the benefit of those who do not understand, let us examine the history of two bluebell bulbs the Writer obtained some years ago for his garden. Inside three years the patch of ground allotted to the bulbs was dug up to rid the ground of bluebells. The following year there were even more bluebells. The digging up of bluebell bulbs continued annually...and carrier bag and wheelbarrow loads have been given away. Finally, bulbs have just been dumped in woodland in a desperate bid to be rid of them! It maybe thought provoking to quote a remark made by a wry colleague of mine during the time that the Writer was trying to persuade the UK Authorities to relax a Tree Preservation Order 'They' he said, 'don't care whether the trees are standing or felled.....as long as they control the matter'.

And then there are Listed Buildings to consider.

37

Undoubtedly, many of these Building are worth preserving [one can preserve buildings and furniture] but the selection of buildings thought to be worthy of Preservation is a subjective matter. Indeed, Land Owners rights to lawfully utilise land for building [even after planning permission has been obtained] or even something as basic as ploughing grassland are often denied by the action of 'Conservationists' demanding 'preservation'. Furtherto, a 'demand' to convert two holes in the ground that earmark the site of two demolished gasometers to the status of an ancient monument is currently reported as being considered by a Government Minister. As such, these examples scarcely seem a suitable matter with which to burden the taxpayer. Besides, some Listed Buildings appear to be what are commonly known as 'follies'....which anyone who knows anything about Planning Controls will tell you would not receive Planning Consent today. And yet here is the State endorsing the expenditure of Public Money to obtain aims which appear at best whimsical and at worst contradictory. Furthermore, the 'proud owners' of Listed Dwellings, having bought with their hard earned cash, seem to be endowed with the task of caretakers. And one may well ask if such undertakings are part of a back door nationlisation scheme.

It would seem that preservation of buildings is not something that governments should burden the poor old taxpayer with. It is better and fairer to place preservation cost of buildings on Public Subscription. Precedent exists in the UK by organisations who fund the preservation of vintage Aircraft, Steam Locomotives and Autocars. Such arrangements ensure that money is not taken by 'force' and wasted on useless examples of antiquity.

* One should bear in mind that pavement or road side trees, usually controlled by Local Councils, ought to be included in the proposed 'rights to light', particularly since trees so placed will eventually inhibit use of desired solar panels for an environmentally friendly hot water system at the writer's Dorset residence.

CHAPTER 6   ³⁸

POSSIBLE SOLUTIONS TO OZONE LAYER DEPLETION
AND ENHANCED GREENHOUSE EFFECT

Clearly, there is a need to protect 'our' environment
from such phenomenon as the depletion of the Earth's
ozone layer and the 'enhanced' greenhouse effect.
However, of the two problems, the enhanced greenhouse
effect is thought to pose the greatest threat to
mankind.

Since ozone is easily manufactured, ie a suitably high
voltage is discharged through oxygen.....it would not
seem beyond the wit of man to generate, containerise and
deliver ozone to the appropriate altitude with an aim of
replacing the destroyed protective layer. Alternatively,
it maybe more efficient to generate ozone 'on site' so
to speak. There is however an immense problem of scale.

As to CFC gas, which is mainly thought to be
responsible for the depletion of the ozone layer, the
vapour is only a hazard when liberated by operating a
'non green' aerosol for example. The domestic
refrigerator, which contains CFC gases cannot pose a
threat unless the sealed source of the gas is broken
without drawing off, recycling or containing the surplus
gases. Never the less, it would seem prudent to find a
harmless substitute and ban or licence the manufacture
of CFC gases.

Since plant life and ultra violet radiation are, within
fairly wide limits, compatible, it would seem humanity
would not suffer too much from the depleted ozone layers
provided that precautions are taken ....like keeping out
of the mid summer midday sun [Ultra Violet transmissions
do not attenuate greatly in the presence of cloud] and
avoiding excessive sunbathing.

Of the two effects, the enhanced green house effect
should, it is thought, cause the more concern in as much
that we all add to the 'layer' each time we breath, turn
on gas, oil, electric or coal heating or indeed utilise

39

a car or aircraft.....or burn fossil fuel for what ever reason. Fears that the 'effect' will melt the polar ice caps and, if achieved, flood vast areas of land is probably valid...and land is a commodity which is already short in supply.

Indeed it maybe too late to avoid some of the consequences of the enhanced green house effect. And then there are those who looking even further ahead, predict that melted polar caps could trigger an ice age.

The general idea that seems to be adopted is that nuclear fuelled electric generating stations will solve, or partly solve, the problem. But as already indicated, the current devices generate radio active waste in a time scale which is much shorter than the material's decay rate. For example, the generally accepted life of a nuclear generating installation maybe thirty years. Dismantling the 'worn out' reactor runs foul of the decay time of the radioactive core of the system. The time taken for this radioactive material to decay to half its original measured value is about one hundred years! In the meantime, the radio active 'mound' continues to be vulnerable to activities of earthquakes, third world dictators bent on retribution for real or imagined slights or the master criminal achieving goals by means of blackmail. And we must remember that during its working period the installation poses a greater potential danger in the form of accidental failure .... which, depending on the exact nature of the fault, could easily pose a threat to all life on earth.* The foregoing omits to take into account the enormous cost of construction of a nuclear power station, a cost which is only exceeded by the act of demolition.

Now the enhanced greenhouse effect, which is causing the present international concern, is caused by a gaseous blanket in the upper regions of our atmosphere. Solar energy finds little difficulty in penetrating this blanket on its Earth bound journey. On reaching the Earths crust this energy changes its wavelength and is,

40

in part, reflected back toward space. However, a greater percentage of this reflected heat is retained now than hitherto due to the increased insulation efficiency this gaseous layer presents to this frequency shifted energy. Since this gaseous blanket is thickening due to increased emissions of, for example, CO_2 from Mother Earth the Earth's average ambient temperature is thought to be increasing.

As any reader who has used a conventional green house may already know, the effect described in the previous paragraph occurs in garden green houses also. It will also be well known that when such a greenhouse overheats one opens a window to allow the surplus heat to escape. It would seem to the Writer that such a mechanism, or similar, is needed with the enhanced greenhouse effect. Although, once again, there is a problem of scale to overcome, but there is also an incentive in as much as our immediate future almost certainly depends upon success. As such, it maybe possible to create a 'gaseous' blanket with a variable heat transmission factor. An example of such a principle maybe seen in a Stirling Engine. This engine creates the required characteristic by means of pressure variations. One can CAREFULLY try the principle by comparing the heat transfer obtained to ones finger by lightly, and momentarily, touching a hot surface and then repeat the experiment in a similar manner but CAREFULLY applying an increased pressure.

A similar result maybe simply imagined or even experienced by comparing the insulation effect of clothes on our body comfort in
a] the dry state
b] a damp state
c] the saturated state which maybe achieved by total immersion, for example, in one of the World's cold oceans.

To return our attention to the upper reaches of our atmosphere. It maybe difficult to increase the pressure or moisture content of a free gas cloud at that altitude

41

which, it must be remembered, is set at a low ambient temperature. However, it might be possible to introduce a gas that will mingle with the culprit gases and which has a higher heat transfer characteristic. Assuming such a gas were to have a temporary life cycle, it maybe possible to regulate the average ambient global temperature. If perchance, some or all of the gases responsible for the 'enhanced greenhouse effect' are ionised, then it maybe possible to repel the gases electrically, ie to open a heat escape vent.

Lastly, and not least, the high altitude blanket of troublesome gases could be combined with a heavier gas...resulting in the combined gases being brought down to earth for capture/conversion/processing.

Hopefully, in spite of the immensity of the problem, some of the proposed solutions for dealing with the 'enhanced greenhouse effect' will prove practicable....and with todays facilities....some maybe. But the general long term solution to societies problem would still seem to be in a drastic reduction of population levels....particularly when a partial earthbound mop up of current CO2 production is estimated by some to require forest plantations equal in area to the continent of Australia!

* Madam Curie died from leukaemia which, it is claimed, was caused by exposure to the few mg of radium refined and discovered by this scientist earlier this century.

CHAPTER 7

42

PLANNING ACTS

Much of the UK and other nation's planning laws seem to fail to stand up to investigation for fundamental reasons. As with Conservation and Tree Preservation Orders [TPO's part of the UK Planning Acts] the concept seems to embrace the Creed of Communism, that is, it denies true ownership. And dissolving the true spirit of ownership cements the bureaucrat into a permanant position...to await the chance to indulge in further expansion. As with TPO's and Conservation Orders, the planning laws seem to permit officialdom to muscle in on what is essentially a private matter. This poking around in other's business seems to extend to members of the public also.....but to a lesser degree than prior to about 1980 when UK Laws were revised and, to a degree, relaxed. However, third party activity, around an intent to erect a home, office block or factory, still appears to resemble a boxing or wrestling match where spectators offer advice to the participants without getting involved in the 'business end' of matters....or though where planning applications are involved the 'advice' maybe of a compulsory nature. But, did someone say, we are a democratic nation. Well, Democracy may be well and good in electing a government or passing an Act in Parliament. But surely one should not soil a principle by excessively employing it to embrace a Communistic type control over private property.

Since one can hardly deny a permanent resident of, for example, the UK, a burial plot, much less a home, [provided it can be paid for] it seems land must be made available for both uses. And since a home and its general shape and size is a personal and subjective matter one would ask how the local planning department, councillors, Department of Environment or the general public ever became involved in its final details. Some maybe tempted to object to the idea of 'a free hand' regarding size, shape and finish of a building.....but comparison of a 'Planned New Town' with the often charming appearance of an 'Old World Village or Market Town' should bring round most critics. Similar argument

can also be applied to factories and office
blocks/shops. After all, we all have our own ideas or
needs regarding detail that makes a building attractive
in architectural/functional terms....and surely no
committee, official or dignitary should be able to claim
the right to over-ride a would be owners 'ideal'.
Especially since UK local authorities have, against the
wishes of owners and occupiers, demolished warm, dry and
economic dwellings known as 'wartime concrete pre-fabs'.
In some cases, these snug homes have been replaced with
damp, cold, and thug infested high rise tower
blocks...sometimes at public expense. However, a scheme
which permitted a free architectural hand, would, if
employed, have to have rules which are clear to all. One
should not have to, as at present, go cap in hand to a
planning authority and ask if this, that or the other is
free of planning consent. This unacceptable state of
affairs is largely caused because of the way the
Planning Acts are presented, amended and written; ie the
Acts are capable of various interpretation. As such, the
present arrangement gives the local authority too much
power over the population and gives scope for
corruption. It may or may not be a mild example of this
undesirable practice where an organisation denotes money
to the council 'for the environment' at the time of
application for planning permission. At any rate, it is
thought that the practice should cease. Any departure
from the foregoing reasoning surely must be repressive,
inefficient, needlessly expensive and may be said to
provide 'jobs for the boys'.

What about the countryside, I can hear the Reader ask.
Well, the point may not arise if the the population is
set at the correct level for the size of the Country
involved. But until this level is reached, a reduced,
but more effective, local planning department could
acquire and allocate land designated for residential,
factory or shop/office block use. Such land once
acquired by planners could be provided with requisite
services, such as water, gas and electricity, and sold
at cost, without additional restriction or covenant, to
members of the public. Centrally imposed, but

44

enforceable rules, would be minimal, but necessary. For example, residential land would not be for any other use...and so on for other types of development. Spacing from boundaries would be minimised according to height of intended dwelling to enable a bungalow to nestle fittingly alongside a three story house... or a multistory block of flats. [Garage space would prevent unduly large areas of wasteland here.] Alternatively, multistorey blocks of flats could be designated to shop/office block zones only. Additionally, a simplified form of Building Regulations which recommended adequately deep foundations to suit the area maybe advisable also. Depth of foundations should not need an Inspectors acceptance since inspection slots could be left in a building's concrete foundations enabling ultrasonic tests to be carried out by any would be purchasers. Obviously, a building with substandard foundations would only be fit for demolition, a right which the original or succeeding owner should have complete freedom to carry out.

Adoption of such schemes would help to permit the necessary repeal of Tree Preservation Orders since it is thought that the main reason for the introduction of such technically misguided Orders [which can result in unacceptable damage] was due to the hyped up protests of owner occupiers who thought, perhaps with some justification, that chain saw activity always precedes the march of the developers. Conservation Orders should have no place in Owner Occupied Land for apart from the introduction of the undesirable Communistic element such Orders prohibit the proper development and care of a garden. Besides, custodians [Councils/Ministries] have been known to override such Orders in spite of prolonged local protests when the desire/need occurs to develop woodland. Therefore these Orders appear to give Local Authorities more powers than is, perhaps, wise or necessary.

Given that the depopulation theme outlined earlier is adopted, and that the ' population run down ' is started, the eventual requirement for 'preservation' of

Daniel Tissington

the countryside and planning controls would be
zero.....or almost. As such, it should eventually be
possible to almost completely disband the Department of
Environment along with the various associated
Commissions. Such organisations seem to rapidly drain
away the taxpayer's money to the depths of a bottomless
pit.....money which has to be earned by the Public
'MANNING' the bench, desk, road, mine or whatever. It is
thought that the public would respond responsibly once
the rationale requiring responsible action is understood
as opposed to the sometimes senseless and damaging dogma
imposed by bureaucrats expressing their interpretation
of Acts which, in themslves, frequently appear to be
misguided.

In the interim period, current planning controls, which
stem from the Town and Country Planning Acts should be
completely rewritten to relax planning matters [as
outlined above] so as to incur minimum formality,
inconvenience and expense to the public. As stated in
Planning Acts Reform Committee's [PARC, founded by
Writer in 1977] submissions to Parliament, the role of
the local planning authority would be drastically
reduced. In short, the main function of a Local Planning
Authority would be to designate and acquire areas of
land for

a] Residential purposes
b] Industrial purposes
c] Shopping/High Rise Flat/ Offices
   and to
d] Oversee simplified Building Regulations
e] Ensure an adequate and economic supply of services
at cost.

Land sales to the public could then proceed at cost, on
demand and without restriction apart from use
designation. Although changes were made to The Town and
Country Planning Acts in the Local Government Planning
and Land Act 1980 they did not adequately reflect PARC's
submission and it is considered pertinent to mention the
document's main points in this work.

46

One may also consider an additional residential catogery of land which permits the erection of non traditional, grade one low cost, prefabricated dwellings for 'first time buyers'. The foregoing facility may reduce or even eradicate the renewed demand [1992] for more Council Houses.

Finally, covenants and restrictions on land imposed by Planning Authorities, especially those preserving rights of view, should be prohibited except as outlined above. Covenants and restrictions imposed by private vendors should be nul and void after a period...say ten years. If our forefathers had similarly indulged their wishes with covenants, half or more of the existing population would not be entitled to their existing homes.

CHAPTER 8   47

WATER DISTRIBUTION

Water distribution in the UK also appears to have got out of hand. It may help the Reader to appreciate what seems to have gone astray by briefly running over the origins of domestic water supplies in this overcrowded Isle.

The Writer, as a boy, witnessed the situation as it was in the UK before the turn of the century. This glimpse of bygone times was achieved by periodic stays at the cottage of the Head Game Keeper to an Oxfordshire Country Estate during summer/autumns of late twenties and early thirties. The Cottage, called Keepers Cottage, was not connected to gas, electricity or water supplies. Oil lamps, candles, outside toilets, wells and wrapped brick 'hot water bottles' were the facilites that existed here!

There were two wells, one supplied drinking water and the other washing water. The two wells were fed from roof drainage [similar systems can be found working today in places] and were interconnected via a sand filter. Life for all that was simple, ordered, clean and joyful. Three or so gallons of clear evaporation cooled drinking water were stored in a giant red brick earthenware pot .....complete with the odd dead earwig at the bottom of the container.

Later on, the remaining part of the 'water story' was pieced together from eye witnesses. Originally, the 'Local Big House' would be provided by a well. Such wells were fed by underground sources where possible and were either located by water diviners or found by digging. If all else failed, the 'hole' was connected to a roof drainage system.

By the turn of the century most of the 'big houses' had a water tank in the attic. These tanks were filled each morning by boys employed to operate a hand pump. As electricity and electrical apparatus became more generally available, the boys were replaced by electric

48

motors, which in turn, operated rotary water pumps. During this period, the Estate Workers generally got their water from a nearby pond, stream or river. Some of the key Estate Workers might have been lucky enough to have their own well.

Eventually, in order to obtain more water storage and water pressure, suitable pressure resists penetration of undesirable foreign materials from external sources at leaky joints and increases water flow, big metal tanks were installed on scaffolding by the Estate Owners. Some of these tanks are still in place today, 1991. In order to maximise the available water pressure these tanks were mounted at the highest available local hill top and the water piped to the 'big house'. Gradually, the Estate Workers, who were normally allocated tied terraced cottages, were given an outside communal stand pipe and tap. Most of these stand pipes have now been replaced with indoor supplies and Local Councils eventually became involved with the Supply by collecting 'water charges.'

In '59, the Writer returned from Canada to the UK and eventually bought a two year old bungalow situated in a quarter acre of Hertfordshire. Rates, including water and sewage, were about thirty pounds per annum. Sometime in the sixties the Council rate was separated from the water charge and a water rate was introduced. The 'new' water rate was not deducted from the Council rate demand, which about that time was revalued, upward, naturally, and both charges continued to increase annually. When the Writer moved to Dorset in 1986 the Hertfordshire outgoings for water, sewage and Council rates had increased to something in excess of eight hundred pounds per annum. Outgoings in Dorset increased from about two hundred and seventy pounds per year in 1986 to something in excess of eight hundred pounds in 1990. The Government review of the Community Charge in 1991 did reduce direct payment to Local Authorities by one hundred and forty pounds per head annually...but the 1991 shortfall was actually paid these Authorities by Central Government. This award to Councils was funded by

49

imposing an extra 2.5% VAT levey on goods/services...ie NO CHANGE in what is seen as an a new 'State Grab' of taxpayers funds! This then is a brief history of water distribution and bureaucratic excesses.

Perhaps only bureaucrats could turn a simple rainwater collection, distribution and disposal system into a multi billion pound complex with even greater increases in sight. Alright, I hear some say, water charges have only increased in line with wages etc, and what about the extra purity of the supply and disposal that exists and the upgrade now required by Brussel's Bureaucrats?

In practice, wages seem to have attempted to follow increases in gas, electricity, rates, mortgage interest rates and petrol charges. [Homes are being repossessed, June'91, at a rate equal to a thousand per week and petrol attracts over 100% tax....and some M P's have the nerve to talk about greedy Oil Companies] Since the point is of central importance to this work the Writer will risk accusations of repetition by reiterating the following. That is, it matters not whether the demand for MORE is made by Central or Local Government, the result is the same.....ie added manufacturing costs per unit. This results in fewer exports, less jobs and general prosperity....unless the increase costs are accompanied by genuine productivity. Under these latter conditions, the plunder from Mother Earth increases along with facilities which enhance population increases...along with more pollution... Therefore it would seem that all sectors should, logically, draw their horns in so to speak. It maybe instructive to complete the 'economic wheel' at this point by showing that no one makes a bigger profit than the working man*...since his symbolic needs amount to a cheese sandwhich and a mac.....and the amount paid in excess of requirement is profit! However, reasonable profit is, generally speaking, necessary in order to fuel the modern world's economic system. But Governments should take less, much less. That is, the absolute minimum necessary to discharge their obligations [as opposed to whims] since the result of more unproductive wages or

50

demand is inflation. That is effectively stealing value from peoples savings,...something most pensioners [apart from UK Civil Servants] can't recoup..and is the equivalent of stealing a squirrels winter hoard of nuts! It seems clear that the 1991 British Government's proposals, that is, to introduce a Poll Tax replacement and The Citizens Charter can only be stop gap measures...since fundamental reform of Local and National Government and their businesses appears to be long overdue!

However, returning to the original subject, one is forced to agree at this stage that the water supply is polluted by nitrates and other fertilisers....some of which are thought to be damaging to human health. But the question is countered as follows. The UK water supply is as good as it has ever been. And since 95% of domestic water is utilised to wash clothes, bodies and to water gardens surely there is no need to supply '100 % distilled tap water' to dwellings [public restauraunts may need special consideration] when currently available cheap filters will remove harmful substances from todays [1991] water supplies. Occupiers of future and existing UK dwellings would be set to benefit if filtered roof water was stored and utilised for drinking. Especially since such a supply would be relatively free of pesticides, fungicides and accidental overdoses of water treatment chemicals as experienced at Camelford. Such a scheme would enhance the Nation's water stocks, reduce the water wastage associated with ' surface run off' due to drought stricken ground and reduce the monopoly still held by privatised Water Companies. Of course, bureaucrats will object to these proposal if only because filters can, if neglected, collect bacteria. Well so can anything...and much of the Public is fed up with bureaucrats who, when permitted by politicians, seem to collect and wastefully divert our money in ever increasing amounts.

Soiled water may perhaps be more thoroughly cleansed' of bacteria by the use of radio-active isotopes, ionisers or even active x-ray or ultra violet generators. The

51

technique may also help iradicate the rat population of
the sewers. However, not all the blame for this 'clean
up' expense can be fairly put on bureaucrats shoulders.
The required level of purification of soiled water waste
could be greatly simplified and cheapened, perhaps by
the utilisation of specialist toilet facilities. For
example, toilet systems which separate human waste and
utilise the process of composting....always assuming
current or future manufactures can show their products
take adequate care of associated virus/heavy metal
content of human sewage. Alternatively, the use of
septic tanks, [not cess pits] might be considered when
population levels are reduced to manageable numbers for
the Country involved. Such a goal might be achieved
sooner rather than later if UK politicians ceased to
pay for human reproduction by means of family
allowances!

* One who receives a wage, a salary or a fee.

CHAPTER 9   52

DISCUSSION/CONCLUSIONS

Having contemplated what are thought to be some of the main points of societies dilemma, [the Writer considers there is more] many of the world's governments and their civil servants do not appear to be suitably aligned to lead humanity into a sustainable life for the period that the sun can continue to radiate its life giving energy. The relevant UK Parliamentary Select Committees, no doubt aided by costly bureaucrats, who are now considering matters dealt with in this work seem to be advocating ways or selecting solutions that permit life to continue as usual by conserving energy. And what, one wonders, will be recommended when further and inevitable increases in population levels exceed present production quotas of pollution in spite of its best efforts with energy economies. Indeed, the organisation of Parliament, and other national governments, appear to have been developed to satisfy other criteria. One reason for this is that many M P's seem to live in lofty White Towers......and when advice is taken it may mainly reflect influential opinion or even civil servants vested interests. It seems that the man in the street' is rarely listened to and never, or hardly ever, consulted. Where irreversible steps are to be taken for the nation, such damaging neglect by elected bodies may be due to lack of understanding, contempt for the man in the street or even plain arrogance. We may quote, for example, the forthcoming 1991 Maastricht summit where' 'The Community' intend to usurp UK Parliamentary Sovereignty. This hard won birthright is held in trust for future generations by the British People whom some of our national leaders think there is no need to consult. Whereas this political claim maybe justifiable with the present holders of Office...who can vouch for their future unknown replacements? Since the right in question is held in trust, it maybe that even a referendum cannot be considered constitutional. It appears logical that in such matters, the people should consider safeguarding the position by humbly requesting H R H Queen Elizabeth II of England that she grant the people an Extraordinary Royal Charter ensuring said

53

powers cannot ever be voluntarily transferred...in
perpetuity. Such safeguards appear reasonable since the
attitude frequently presented by successive national and
local goverments appears to gently portray the dogma of
vote, pay up and shut up. Of course, some of the
assorted opinions held by the man in the street will
need discarding....but the man 'at the coal face' is
often practical [mostly by necessity] and therefore may
know a thing or two which would be beneficial to the
world if taken into account. However, most of the input
from such sources appears to be discarded and it is
thought that this anomaly should be remedied.

It is easy to make empty claims. But the Writer has
found that many MP's fail to reply to correspondence or
avoid group meetings designed to discuss problems that
stem from legislation which seems to be technically
misguided or incomplete. Therefore, evidence or
indications which tend to reveal the truth are mostly
lost or never formulated. Alternativly, correspondence
is redirected to ministries where such legislation was
initially drafted. Replies which are then received
sometimes seem out of touch, probably because the sense
of the complaint is misunderstood. On occasions a
ministry may fob off the constituent on a point which is
thought to be undermining its own position. In fact, if
the legislation complained of is faulty, surely it is
for the MP to investigate and attempt to instigate
corrective measures however unpopular these may appear
to be. Of course, the reasons for such strange and
unacceptable behaviour on the part of some MP's maybe
because they are not sure if they are having their legs
pulled [nobody knows it all] or if they are being
manoeuvred. It maybe that they even consider the effect
a given intervention will have upon their Selection
Committee and their personal subsequent future. Or it
may simply be that there is no 'blame free' way in
existance of raising matters about which they are not
sure. In any event the problem of lack of local and
national accountability is too vital to ignore and ways
round the matter have to be found.

54

Local newspapers will sometimes hound an MP or Councillors who will not meet Constituents 'round the table'. But it seems, that in most cases, it depends on the political hue that the MP or journal supports. So whereas the Parliamentary and Local Government system is more humane than some totalitarian regimes [it will not shoot or roll tanks over protesters] it will, on far too many occasions, ride over the people in a gentle manner to perpetuate outdated, wasteful, generally unwanted or even suicidal schemes. And the initiating officer presumably wins promotion for the outragous antic.

For example, investers who are willing to take risks with their money should be protected from fraud, and one would think this the task of the Fraud Squad. Since no one can claim 100% success in investment matters, what are the various protection boards set up by UK Government at taxpayer's expense supposed to do? Recent case histories may cause one to believe they are expected to act as State Insurance Agencies for unlucky or unwise investors....with taxpayers money. Naturally, government schemes need funding...and it must be difficult to know how to raise necessary taxes. But excesses in this matter appear to lead to the need for tax collectors to 'stand over the deceased'. In some cases, refusal to grant probate until the tax man is paid off results in the need for the bereaved to raise expensive loans...in order to finance what often appears to be wasteful government expenditure.

All too frequently, council/government officials, police and M P's 'cannot help the citizen' and the civil courts are difficult to use....and yet these public bodies seem, on numerous occasions, to be able to act in no uncertain way against the citizen. And it just maybe that there are two different ways of framing legislation.

Although it may seem ungrateful to protest in this way [we are, in the main, able to house and feed ourselves] the outlook for continuity is not thought to be 'set fair'. And noting the numbers of civil servants employed

55

by politicians, the amount of taxpayers money spent, and wasted, by Parliament/Local Authorities and their equivalence the world over, it is thought the world's population is entitled to expect a less short sighted scenario than currently seems to exist.

Finally, it seems that the 'bottom line' of each of societies main problems looked at in the preceding text indicate that a need exists to reduce human number by at least half initially*...and to reduce the numbers of civil servants by a much much greater proportion.

* The ratio of the earth's 'haves' [the main polluters] to the world's 'have nots' [who do not add much to the sum of humanities global damage in terms of pollution] can be estimated as approximately 1:1 since China and India currently contain about 1.75 billion souls out of a total world's population of 5 billion people. The forgoing indicates that Mother Earth, which is currently unable to cope with plundering of resources and resultant pollution, MAY BE ABLE to support 2.5 billion individual Homo sapiens at todays western standards of living.

CHAPTER 10

SOME RECOMMENDATIONS

The Writer recommends the contents of this Work to Governments...where the contents are applicable. But in particular, it would seem that many National Government's need to drastically reform civil servant departments which appear overmanned and too departmentalized. A need also exists to insist that UK civil servants use straightforward language to make Acts or frame legislation easily and unarguably understood. Additionally it would be commendable if UK Ministries were made to desist from continously commissioning expensive repeat adverts extolling the virtues of their 'free' expertise or exhorting the public to comply with x, y and z or else.......

The practice of achieving knowledge or data from possibly dangerous experimental tasks in peace time, such as exposure to nuclear bomb tests or radiation, should be passed to well paid volunteers who are given known facts and possible results of participation.

Government's elected members should give similar or more attention to complaints from the 'Man in the Street' regarding proposed or existing legislation such as is usually reserved for smoothing away complaints concerning procedural and social injustices or hardships.

That proposals or complaints about technically misguided, unworkable or incomplete UK legislation, based on knowledge or experience should, as a right, on request by a constituent, be filed under the relevant Act/File on a goverment computer. The data, which should be privileged, ie free from exposure to libel, would be held for use by a select committee as well as individual elected members in an effort to retain and collate information with a view to extending, updating, refining or scrapping legislation. Where necessary, a select committee should be able to summon the named source for additional data, confirmation etc. The data [less names at option of originater] should also be available to the public, press and television companies in order to inform the public and safeguard against observed government indifference/apathy.

It is thought that powers given exclusively to police/local authorities/ministries should be reviewed and, where possible, should be made available for use by any member of the public....since authorities frequently seem to avoid using these powers for the good of society and often apply them when they wish to 'show their authority'.

The UK Government should also consider revising the Planning Acts in line with proposals given in Chapter 7....an action which may be sufficient to permit VAT levels to be reset to 15%!

That all National and Local Governments should publish and make freely available detailed annual departmental/ministerial running costs, individual expenses and manning levels.

That if GB's friends in the Common Market cannot understand

a] why GB's Government and large numbers of GB's population wish to limit the Community to an Association of Trading Partners and

b] the Government's hesitation to blindly concede to other members requirements for European Political Union

we must remind ourselves of additional adverse examples of federalism provided by USSR, Yugoslavia etc. And then UK Government surely must give the public the opportunity of withdrawal from membership of the European Community by means of a referendum that we may resume traditional trading links with the USA and the Commonwealth. Perhaps the Community eventually would wish to join a reformed GB...assuming that the bureaucratic monster now in the throes of being created, with its hoards of civil servants, manage in the longer

58

term to avoid causing the demise of humanity.

Alternatively, in the interests of the environment, economy and reducing restraint on an already over governed land, UK Parliament must surely consider disbanding after relinquishing all or more of its sovereignty to Brussels.

NB In the interests of halting the threatened environmental disaster, the remarks about hoards of civil servants and the urgent need to reduce their numbers is thought to apply equally to most developed nations.

Care should be exercised where statistical analysis of any sort is offered as weight to adopt or reject an Act, scheme or point since much depends upon compilation of data and use of same. Such results are apt to mislead and are easily misinterpreted. One may relate, by way of example, the tale about the fearful airline passenger who packed a bomb in his suitcase because a statistician had informed him the chances of boarding an aircraft with two differently sourced bombs aboard was nil!

Parliament should safeguard against enormous increases in cost that usually accompanies reorganisation...since the cost of most official tasks is far too high already and bureaucrats, either from lack of knowledge or from self interest, seem ever ready to increase them!

UK Government should also consider a simple list of protected animals, plants and birds, to be revised annually, and displayed in Police Stations and Post Offices. Species should be added or deleted as necessary. Currently, for example, magpies should be deleted from such a list.

Printed by Q-print, Ashley Lane, New Milton, Hants.

REF 5

A PROPOSAL FOR A WRITTEN CONSTITUTION Jan: '07

[i]

INDEX
----

i]   INDEX

ii]   INTRODUCTION

P1   RATIONALE for ARTICLE 1 and RATIONALE for ARTICLE 2

P2   RATIONALE for ARTICLE 3 and RATIONALE for ARTICLE 4

P3   RATIONALE for ARTICLE 5

P4   RATIONALE for ARTICLE 6

P5   RATIONALE for ARTICLE 7

P6   RATIONALE for ARTICLE 8

P7   RATIONALE for ARTICLE 9

P8   RATIONALE for ARTICLE 10 and RATIONALE for ARTICLE 11

P9   RATIONALE for ARTICLE 12 and RATIONALE for ARTICLE 13

[ii]

Herewith, as promised, is the proposed written Constitution, now formally at Issue 3, dated January '07 & which originated as a stated intent in a letter dated 10th July 01 to Ms M Moran MP. Its aim is to achieve an all Party Parliamentary agreement for the document to exist as a written & enforcable agreement between Parliament & the People of GB because the present System is unaffordable AND doesn't work!.

An opening draft outline of first of proposed clauses of a written CONSTITUTION to protect the population of GB from omissions/excesses of the EU, Parliament & their agencies was attached as an APPENDIX in a letter to Ms M Moran MP dated 16th March 02. This was followed by Iss 1 of said document on 21st April '02. There is need for this work because Parliamentarians of all parties fail to properly review the results of their handiwork as it affects GB 's Citizens ... they protest when one of their members is caught in rules they have set ...but expect the public at large to poke up with the mayhem they have caused .... until, as stated , one of their own are affected!! Of consequence, more unworkable bureaucracy is stacked atop of existing bureaucratic legislation.The result begats fraud by double charging, waste of public effort, vandalism even death & public protest is far too often to no avail. Detailed obsevations show one LA will react to a given complaint whereas another will not & will feign horror at suggestions that they should. Reaction to identical problems even vary within a given LA ....which seems to indicate that it depends who is complaining! Most of the unacceptable practise has increasingly taperd into use from the 'fifties' to recent times. And although temporary relief from problems is sometimes achieved by means of a quiet word in some Official's ear, that is when an MP or Councillor take their duty seriously, without amendment of legislaton, the basic problem continues Nationwide, & ultimately re- occurs locally!

It maybe some of the following corrections will override GB's legislation such as the T&CPAs or EU directives. However, it is thought that in the interests of GB's survival as a livable Sovereign State means that where ever the requirements outlined in the ongoing Articles clash with other directives & legislation, that the said directives & legislation must be altered or be renegotated. If alteration or re negotiation of the offending EU directives is not possible then a UK referendum on withdrawal from the EU must be considered as a safe alternative because EC trade with GB is assured under the Treaty of Rome. In any event, such a referendum is thouht to be owed to the public of GB since the people were initially conned by PM T Heath's referendum on the matter which asked if GB should join the EU TRADING BLOCK....& we, the public, are being sucked & conned into a Federal EU STATE. There is no doubt that such a proposal will be dismissed by some for reasons of dogma or without further thought. But the principle of allowing remotely placed individules to control or oversee the requirements of the owner of an asset such as a Sovereign State or a house is a flawed bad joke which no intellegent person can justify in terms of theory or practice! However, it is admitted that this document is composed with the partial benefit of hindsight.....but some of the matters raised were predicted by the writer in the 1990. * *

No apology is rendered for points that some might dismiss as ' trivial' since so called irritations can, taken to extremes, have expensive or even fatal repercussions. It is thought that the right to by- pass LA's to terminate a nuisanse via the offices of the small claims court would improve & reduce the lot /costs of/to the people. Such appeals to the Court is seen as a last resort following a 'chat over the garden wall' & or a non abusive letter. The writer is also mindful of the fact that whereas that when one sets out to drain a swamp it maybe difficult to remember this fact when one finds oneself up to the arm pits in crocodiles!

ARTICLE 01   RATIONALE-: It has come to my notice that some Local Authorities have banned the flying of the Union Jack, the Standards of St George, St Andrew & St Patrick. Furthermore, some of GB 's ministries refuse to accept the word "English" in official documents'.

-
-
    ARTICLE 01- CLAUSE 1   In CLAUSE 01, we the public of GB acquire a right as an owner or tenent of land or property to fly the Union Jack, the Standard of St George, St Andrew & St Patrick from any private property/land at any time between the hours of sunrise & sunset without let or hinderence, but subject to following provisos. The owner or tenent of such land or property has the unchallenged requirement to to allow third parties to fly the said Standards always subject to the overriding requirement that sign posts, traffic signals are not obstructed from view of intended users & safety is accorded to GB's public from the ravages of flying bunting.

-
-
    CLAUSE 02-   UK citizens further acquire the right of choice to describe him or herself on any government or government agency document, or any other document, as British, English, Irish, Scotish or Welsh as the case may truely be & that pardon be granted retrospectively to   any convicted British Subject for offending by insisting on describing his/herself, correctly, as English or whatever .

ARTICLE 02- RATIONALE : Owner Occupiers, Owners & Tenants of Business, Manufacturing , Farm Premises or Outhouses enjoy zero or near zero power to protect their properties from the trespass of forest trees foliage & their rooting systems that are too close to their property. See letter addressed to Ms M Moran MP dated 16th March, 02. Protection is also needed to protect storm & sewer drains. There is also a need to protect the person from physical damage or even death from forest trees or trees that are too close to said properties /appendages that it is impossible for the tree to fall without causing damage to property or inhabitants of said property. There is also a need to observe & prevent the relationship occuring between the necessity of excessive farm use of pesticides, fungicides where this is due to high tree planting desities [an occurance which can cause festations of fungal/insect destruction to all other plant life; a classic example being the destruction of Elm trees in GB] . . ... & to uphold the preservation of the UK population from indirect & direct contamination such as cancer from said sprays.

This paragraph extends to Owner Occupiers, Landowners , Tenents & owners of other structures to acquire the ability to rapidly & economically protect property or land from squatters & burglers or persons who break & enter. There is also the matter of personal safety from intruders in the form of burglers/break & entry persons who maybe armed with firearms/screwdrivers & knives..since our political masters & the Police are more adequately protected than the rest of the population. And ordinary members of the Great British Public must be protected to at least the same degree as pre mentioned Officals from a physical & legal standpoint .

There is need to protect the Owner Occupier from being 'converted to Council Tenants' where the management of privately owned property is taken over by LA's via TPO's, Conservation Orders & Listed Building Status. It should be noted the 'rental' is occuring from ever increasing, fraudelant & grossly excessive council tax demands. Giving control over Soverign States or private property to remote parties/people such as Commissioners/ Councillors results in severe frustration, possible damage/danger, severe rundown or even destruction of the asset concerned because of political dogma, disinterest, low standards, political correctionness, treachery ...or even gross ignorance !

-
    . ARTICLE 02 CLAUSE 03   grants Owner Occupiers, Tenants, Owners of Business, Manufacturing & Farm Premises an affordable, no nonsense right through the Courts [see Article 12] to secure the removal of forest trees growing on neighbouring ground that are situated within the radial distance for damage to building foundations as described by ETR's CI/SIB[16]WPL dated April 1999, Page 3, Table 1. Some [hopfully to be specified by author of said report] modification is to be permitted on the said ETR document
-
    where the root trespass is committed on a non clay based soil. Furthermore, forest trees should not be permitted to grow to a height, which, on falling from the effects of age, disease, storm or wind will cause damage to any property which is leagally occupied by human beings for purposes of residence, business, manufactureing processes, stock
-
    tending or storage purposes. The protection would also extend to protect garages,empty or otherwise. Roots of forest tree/trees removed for purposes descibed in this

WP1

- paragraph should be treated with sodium chloride or other suitable chemicals such as diesel fuel oil to prevent the tree re-offending by sprouting new growth.

- CLAUSE 4 gives a no nonsense right to be accorded to Landowners, Owner Occupier or Tenents & other property owners through the Courts to remove squatters speedily &
- cheaply from any building or outhouse through the medium of a near automatic Court Injunction.[see ARTICLE 12] The Court Order should be coupled with immediate Police co-operation to rid the property/land so affected. That is, the absence of a paid up rent book & a valid tenant or use agreement results in immediate vacation of said property or land.

- CLAUSE 05 There is a right granted, under Clause 05 to a legal occupant of a property or outbuilding to use force of any sort to protect his /her person & other legal occupants or occupiers or users of said property from the ravages or plunder of a burglar, burglers or break & entry personel. In order to protect the legal occupiers, whilst inside said abodes, business manufacturing or outbuilding facility from an 'armed' or unarmed intruder or intruders, gas sprays capable of long range knock out similar to the type carried by Police Constables should be leagally available for use when required.... with no penalty what-so-ever for employment of said spray regardless of results. There is obvious need to repeal The Human Rights Act!

- -
- Clause 06 also requires planted density of trees to be controlled to prevent the excessive entertwining of foliage in areas where arable farming is practiced. Relaxation of the restriction should be taperd as the site of afforestation is sited more northernly...ie away from farmland &areas of high population levels.

- Clause 07 requires the repeal of Orders such as TPO's, Conservation Orders & Listed Building Status relating to any Privately owned Dwellings, Business & Manufacturing Premisis, Outhouses or Garages.

- ARTICLE 03 RATIONALE-:: 'The EUROPEAN ARREST WARRENT' to which the UK Government has given its agreement *without parliamentary debate* allows a European Magistrates the right to arrest a British Citizen on British soil with unsupervised foreign police under laws which do not apply in GB. The Bill is reported to allow terrorist suspects & other British Subjects to be jailed indefinitely without trial. This Bill appears to allows the EU & The State 'too much power & it is fair to say that if there is need for for such draconion powers that need has been caused by daft agreements which surrender our boarders to Brussels for example.. ' This & similar 'excesses of power' granted the EU/UK such as the ability to criminalise a trader for quantifying amounts of a sale of vegetables, or other goods sold by weight, other than in grams should be repealed & official pardon granted to traders already so branded. The rationale is further supported by a report that vegetables are sold by the pound in Brussels street markets.

The requirement of CLAUSE 9 is that EU/GB law should not ban the display of weight in Grams or indeed Grains or Carats or Pounds since a quantity of goods weighing one pound equates to 454 grams or 2270 carats or 7006 grains. That is, if the quantity is properly quantifiable, no crime or fraud has been committed...anymore than the quaint, or even idiotic, practice of costing barrels of UK produced crude oil in dollars is in anyway criminal.

- ARTICLE 3 CLAUSE 8 will require the UK Citizen is granted the protection of Habeaus Corpus when arrested, by whom so ever, on British soil. Clause 8 also permits an extended time period [now believed to be 30 days under current law] above & beyond the period of detention allowable under Habeaus Corpus of suspects thought guilty of an act of terrorism where sufficent evidence is or maybe available, but is awaited to enable a charge to be brought to bear under the auspices of an approprate Act of Terrorism .

- CLAUSE 9 also prohibits the criminalisation of a British Subject for non fraudulent operations such as selling weighed goods in measured standards other than metric & this will operate retrospetively.

ARTICLE 4 RATIONALE-: Population levels of Mother Earth are too high. Ref Classical Environmental Folly Ed 5 [available at major UK Reference Libraries]. In particular, GB is listed among those nations with the greatest population density of any Nation including China & India. But UK Government is attempting to address the problem by a 'price/regulation war on motorists' to fund a public transport system & heaven knows what else at a rate of income amounting to £1000or so /second & by building high density housing estates to house uncontrolled immigration levels. The problem of feeding these overcrowded worldwide populations is not being properly addressed in spite of recent claims that genetic mapping of rice , which, for exmple, enables increases storage life, yields & nutrision of the commodity. One ignores the inability to feed world wide & GB's increases of population due to immigration or excessive large families in the face of unstoppable climate cycles of global warming/ice ages at OUR PERIL. * To do so risks attracting accusations of reckless direliction of responsibility. Furthermore, the British Government is inexplicable permitting unlimited numbers of Asylum Seekers to enter GB...thus adding to the problem of overpopulated GB ...WITHOUT REFERENCE TO THE BRITISH PEOPLE re: OTHER OPTIONS . In response to public protest GBs' Government intends [sometime]to introduce medical examinations for immigrants but will not bar those who fail it with incurable complaints! Furthermore, it is clear the complaints re the management or government of GB must not be inhibited by censorship imposed by so called 'political correctness' or 'over the top observance' of sensibilities.

-
-
- ARTICLE 4 CLAUSE 10 requires the British Public be given a informed choice, through the mechanisms of a referendum, of halting, limiting & or reducing the UK levels of population by means of birth control & limiting or halting the acceptance of more Asylum Seekers versus the option of increasing the levels of UK population levels by all specified means. CLAUSE 4 will put an end to further Asylum Seekers entering GB until the matter has been properly debated and a referndum has been held to find the opinion of the registered nationals of GB . The choices will be-:

-
- A] No further immigrants
- B] Further immigrants permitted at the rate of 1, 2 or 3 thousand persons per year.
-
- If the decision of the referendum is B] then this action will be reviewed by further & repeat five year referenda as specified in CLAUSE 10 above.

-
- CLAUSE 11 prevents the possibility of immigrants converting GBs established way of life to carbon or near copy of a system which the immigrant is seeking asylum from. Each immigrant will be required to learn the English language to an agreed standard, take a course giving an Introduction to UK Customs, take a loyalty pledge to Britain & the Union Flag before taking up British Citizenship. Applicant Immigrants suffering incurable disease will not be allowed to take up resident status in GB.

-
- CLAUSE 12 prmits all immigrants, Nationalized & Indigenous UK citizens to marry overseas parteners of their choice...but they will then be required to take up residence in the country of their oversea spouses, whom, in the interests of UK population limitation will not be able to acquire UK citizenship.

-
- CLAUSE 13 requires that Immigrants, when permitted as in B above, must apply for acceptance or entry visas to the UK at the British Embassy in country of their origin since all other attempts to enter GB will be prevented at point of attempted entry.

-
- CLAUSE 14 requires any attempt at unauthorized entry to GB , ie without entry visas, will attract penalising fines for transgressors & on the carrier/carriers.

ARTICLE 5 Rationale-: This Article requires that the British People be granted a retrospective referendum to accept or reject UK Parliamentry or Foreign Based Legislation, including EC Legislation, involving Great Britian's 'management' that cannot be readily revoked by a simple Act of Parliament. Such choice would be retrospective & includes the surrendering of past or future UK Parliamentary authority over UK Taxation, UK Currency, UK Armed Forces [except for specific & temporary engagements against Terrorists & other forces engaged in hostile acts against the UK or its close allies such as the Commonwealth or the USA or the EU] The British people will also be granted referendum on the restoration or retaining of existing or replaced UK practice by other standards such as the metric system where such changes are designed to replace rather than existing in a parallel form alongside UK standards.

There is need also to set a 'quorum' & an acceptance percentage vote relating to accepting referendum results.

-
- ARTICLE 5 CLAUSE 15 ensures that 'drip by drip' errosion of UK soverignty is halted or at least formally accepted by its population by granting referendum regarding acceptance or rejection of standards, such as the metric system, currancy units, amalgamations of armed forces, judicial systems & Regional Assemblies [which are believed to be scheduled to report to Brussels] that are intended to replace or do replace, or partially replace, British Institutions or Standards. The requirements of Clause 5 should not interfere with acceptance of parallel arrangements which do not override, replace or partially replace existing or past British practice, custom or law.

-
- Clause 16 sets requirements for acceptance or validity of all future UK referenda-:.
- There shall be a minimum of 65% turnout of elegible voters after spoilt ballot papers have been discounted. Acceptance of the motion will require a minimum of 55% of total partisipant's 'ayes'.

-
- Clause 17 requires that the alteration, amendment or additions to this Document, once accepted by Parliament, be subject to the requirements of referendum as specified in Clause 5
-

ARTICLE 6 Rationale-: UK Government will constantly review costs of governing the UK since all forms of government is an overhead. As such... costs should be minimised..... since the results of omission cause [depending on minipulation of interest rates] increases in the cost of goods & depresses the value of the pound as workers seek extra wages to pay for increased taxes or....holds steady the cost of wages & goods. Either way, this is a hidden form of transferring a citizen's wealth to the State. Carried to excess, the policy is a recipe for economic & political collapse... as seen in the USSR. The EU & New Labour is adopting such antics with its expensive tastes, fraud & lavish pay /expenses policies which cost GB £ 1.5 Million PER HOUR, repeat £1.5 Million per hour. There is further unspecified increase in costs due to the enlargement of the EU as agreed in DEC '02. In return , the UK get an unacceptable fishing policy, [ie losses such as food for the impending ice age, UK Fisherman's jobs, British food source & UK income from sale of surplus fish] CAP [which doubles each UK household' s food bill] blocked channel ports, burned lamb exports, illigal refusal to buy British Beef & unlimited number of restrictive directives which is leading to totalitarianism &, by definition, the enslavement of its people! All this makes a nonsense of official UK claims that UK government costs about 40% of GNP.....especially since in '84/'85 LA's were 'accredited' of spending ' 25% of GNP & employing about 14% of GB's workforce .[Source DoE Leaflet 1986 ENV1 J012ON & is currently 25% of workforce] Therefore, the serious pruning of costs, almost non existing at present, is an urgent necessity & an ongoing task, since most Local Authorities [including County Authorities] & Whitehall have based or added their existing excessive tax demands on previous requirements which in many cases no longer require funding or obtain other funding....ie double charging. For example, sewage charges come to mind, the funding is now the responsibility of other authorities, companies & agencies such as Water Authorities ...but the amounts were never removed from most LA Budgets. Some specific details are given in the Writer's 'Report Requesting Parliament for Council Tax Reduction', dated September 1998 [CC Ms M Moran MP] & show that a band D property which was rated at £25 per Annum [inclusive of sewage charges] in 1959 had outgoimgs due to council tax & double charging of +3600% in 1998 compared to RPI [all items] increase of 550%. Further checks reveal an 8% per annum increase to year '01/'02 which was sheduled to produce 'capping'. PM please note. Other specific & generalised examples of double charging are given in a letter to Ms M Moran MP dated September 2001. Much of this unwarrented income is then wasted or disposed of by extravagant upgrading of expenses & pension subcriptions allocated to elected or appointed officials/staff ; & cannot therefore provide for improved services. [There would be less need of this document if this was not as stated] Recent examples are-:Leader of Bedfordshire CC could have wages almost doubled & another 49 councillors could net another £3200 expenses ...most of whom have full time jobs! Bang goes another £ 0.5 Million. See Luton & Dunstable on Sunday dated 24th March,'02. In addition ,all 49 councillors around the County will have their allowences hiked from £5253 to £8500 per year. These rises are recommended by an independant panel. The Beds Police Authority voted to double its allowances & the Chairman will be entitled to £20,000 per annum year whilst ordinary members will suffice on £8000. SEE Luton & Dunstable on, Sunday 25th Nov. 01. This on five [5] meetings per year! Many of the TBPA Board are councillors & most have full time jobs! The public have no say in these excessive 'hand outs or should it be take outs' & it is no wonder that some of my colleagues cannot distinguish between Council Tax Demands & 'A Protection Racket' Many of Town Hall/County Council charges are merely self pepetuated budget blow ups [eg council tax relief which is subsidised by Whitehall from general taxation] and both sets of Authorities & their responsibilities/budgets should be pruned to rationalise council tax demands. Additionally, & equally unacceptably, it is believed many UK government agencies are structured as inverted pyramids...ie ten cowboys in charge of a single Indian! The Fraud Squad, who were made aware of said double charging took no action because it was their written belief that no one had committed an offence. If this finding is correct remedial legislation is obviously required. ...but what is the current status of Ministers, MP's Councillors, Resident Association Chairman, Media Interests, Civil servants & government agenecy employees who have ignored pleas for help in this matter? Aiding & abetting comes to mind! [Fraud Squad please note.]

- ARTICLE 6 CLAUSE 18 requires that the Public Accounts Committee & the The Audit Commission be amalgamated & restructured as an independant all Party organisation with portfolio which investigates complaints from where-so-ever regarding waste, overmanning, double charging & costly bureacratic practice. The committee should consist of 10% of ordinary members of the public with priority, where ever possible, given to persons issuing complaints under consideration. The Committee's duties need to consist of rooting out double charging , other fraud, waste, bureaucratic waste & overmanning due to duplication of effort in UK local , county , national government, Brussels & UN, NATO organisations by means of on going monitoring of all UK government activity.

-
- CLAUSE19 requires back dated action of findings of the Audit Committee, who blamed Council inefficency on weak Councillors, overpaid management & accused LA of wasting £1Billion per year. [seeTimes Jan 11th '95] This Clause requires the updating of that work .

-
- CLAUSE 20 requires the reorganised committee to publish & look at past & future complaints from whom so ever....especially when made by the media & ordinary members of the public. Examples of this are Times 15th May '94 which prints an article stating Hi Tech spending to the tune of £4 billion failed to cut numbers of Whitehall staff , a feat which contrasts with British Telecom who reduced staff levels from 250000 to 150000 after the '81 privatisation scheme. The matter 'A REPORT REQUESTING PARLIAMENT FOR COUNCIL TAX REDUCTION' dated September 1998 & letter to Ms M Moran MP dated September 2001 & the rationale for CLAUSE 18 will also be investigated & acted upon.

-
- Clause 21 requires parliament to instruct the restructured committee to publish findings & publically recommend corrective action to halt any malpractice including redirection of policy. Where possible, recommendations involving rationalisation of the offending Office/Authority should be given & published with an aim to save expenditure & refund taxpayers via reduced tax demands.

-
- CLAUSE 22 requires parliament to publish actions & non actions relating to the combined commitee findings.

-

ARTICLE 7 RATIONALE-: Past & present examples of gross Parliamentary mismanagement include UK part in slavery/denial of a parliamentary election vote to woman/misleading the UK public over the UK role in Europe/double charging on Local/National taxation/failing to ensure the safety of the Maria Cowells' of this Nation/plus the introduction of the European Arrest Warrent which will instil fear, deter free speech/enslave the population/policies on immigration of O/S immigrants in this overcrowded isle [a policy that will reduce this already overcrowded Island into a hotbed of ghettos since we are already encroaching on the green belt to house overseas visitors, ...an option fiercely opposed over the last half century when required for the benefit of the indigenous population .....introducing incurable diseases & financial ruin due to welfare payments to unfortunate immigrants who may be facing in their homeland similar conditions that GB faced not so long ago when children pulled loaded coalcarts in coal mines]

As a Nation we have fought & worked our way out of these conditions. And we do not want to return to them due to our political leaders inexplicable actions. Parliament cannot [& should not] turn around on a sixpence... but it shouldn't take half a century, or more, to deal with each & every justified complaint about its appalling mismanagement & failures to the UK people it represents!

There is an overriding factor relating to all listed [& non listed] cases of mis-management. It is not entirely due to watered down or unsatisfactory legislation...or though this is part to blame [the matter is expanded in ARTICLE 8...& it is thought to be mainly due to the fact that the Public Sector Workers & Elected Representitives are not having to face dismissal for failing to to fully address their responsibilitiesin the short term ...or at all...& they seem unable to put themselves in the position of the legitimate protester! They also seem to have forgotten that they are here to serve the public of GB. Matters of State[Major & Minor] are frequently ignored or dealt with in a 'half baked' manner' because Parliamentary Government is rarely dismissed by back bencher MPs....it would destroy their income! The Monarchy can dismiss Parliament....but the possible 'backlash' may make prudence a preferred or even wise option. Therefore, the long suffering public only have a brief opportunity at the polls to exert any political influence at all...even when their MPs [& Councillors] are causing irreparable & or even terminal damage to OUR Nation when barely into a five year term! And apart from the fact the people ought to have more say in the affairs of the Nation, something is needed to substitute the proposal which 'neuters the second chamber'.

- ARTICLE 7 CLAUSE 23 gives the UK Public a right to trigger the dismissal of Parliament by employing the admirable example afforded by The Sun Newspaper with its recent petition to Parliament regarding the problem with 'out of control immigration' & which polled over half a million protest signatures. This ARTICLE bestows the public right of a petition & 'follow up' petition [A public right is thought to be necessary since the Media is a money making concern but its power brings responsibilities which are frequently not fully discharged perhaps because it fears to lose readers, listeners or viewers by expressing other's views as 'its own' or incurring a charge of libel] by disgrunted voters resulting in an irretrievably trigger to dismissal Parliament by Royal Proclaimation if it were deemed by protesters that the correction requested was ignored or dealt with in an ineffective wishy washy manner. Matters raised in the reader column would start the process of a newspaper poll & the forum would be free of lible action except where matters raised were completely & obviously malicious. It is required that MPs assist their constituants in getting unresolved matters of concern into letter columns...a task which is frequently 'avoided' by not following up a 'we'll see' remark because it is thought, of loyalties to 'The Party'. A qualifying petition would require a number of signatures that might be expressed as a proportion of the participating journals' circulation. A guide to this percentage might be be obtained from The Sun's claim of a record response re; their immigration poll where a figure of 400,000 was reached....assuming a circulation of ten million .... say 4%. The fear of de-stabilising UK Government, as the Italians' experienced last century, should not occur as the matter of an Administration's continuity is firmly in its own hands !

- CLAUSE 24 prevents the use of Clause 23 for use to seek pay or award increases for protest groups such as pensioners or trade unions.

ARTICLE 8 RATIONALE-: Most of the Public Sector Workers find innumerable reasons for not complying with requests such as they are out of funds/have no legal powers/ have to consider others rights [even for neighbours from hell] Personal & documented experience of the writer shows that where powers are subsequently granted to LA's & Councillors to remedy an previous complained of nuisance they sometimes individually say 'WE DONT ISSUE ASBO's ON THAT BASIS' .... even though it can be shown other LA's comply in similar cases! What this results in is high taxes, waste, damage, frustration, run down residential estates, injury....or even death. Brussels, Whitehall, & LAs need their responsibilities 'cut back' so that the public gets a first class service at a reasonable cost...ie without being 'double charged'. The proposal to put LA's revenue on an income tax basis merely appears to be a dodgy way of 'resetting the datum line' to enable another 'Toad of Toad Hall' increase in Council Tax demands!
T&CPAs are first in line for rewriting & although there may be many ways of doing this some possibilities are given in pages 14/16 in the writers' 'A REPORT REQUESTING PARLIAMENT FOR COUNCIL TAX REDUCTIONS' & 'CLASSICAL ENVIRONMENTAL FOLLY', ED 5. [See Copy Ed 5 in major UK Ref: Libraries] Further possible LA economies in

collecting domestic rubbish are outlined in a letter to Ms Moran dated September 2001. County Halls would be more efficient if meaningful cut backs were imposed on Social Services & the service was focused by directing efforts of the reduced force by ensuring protection of the Maria Cowells' of this Nation. PM /Mayor Livingstone & Ch Ex Westminister Council were informed that it can be shown that central London's roads are utilised to about 30% of capacity...but congestion charges prevail without further investigation! See letter to Ms M Moran dated September '02.

Elected & Public Sector Workers should give full consideration to understanding the fact that harsher restriction on residents becomes increasingly essential as the density of residential dwellings increases. This simple fact increases the validity of the case given in 'Classical Environmental Folly' for reducing UK population levels! Other suggestions appear in P12/13 of the writer's 1998 REQUESTING PARLIAMENT FOR COUNCIL TAX REDUCTION. The final observation of the section dealing with Dorset County Council shows 25% of its total budget being awarded to Students, Community Care & Third Parties....which prompts the question 'Is this CC an Authority or a Charitable Trust? The handout requires severe cut back.

- ARTICLE 8 CLAUSE 25 grants the UK Public the right to trigger the dismissal of the elected bodies of a Local Council or County Hall by means of a 'follow up poll' held in the principle local paper, TV or Radio Station in a near carbon copy of ARTICLE 7 CLAUSE 23.. The authorising body, who will substitute for the Monarchy would be the Lord Lieutenant of the County who will be granted the power of dismissing the said Authority by authority of the local electrate newspaper poll. The final action can only be taken after exhausting a simplified vertion of Local Government Act of 1972, if applicable, which allows a Citizen who has filled the necessary requirements to call a referendum which binds an LA.
-
- CLAUSE 26 prevents the use of CLAUSE 25 to seek direct pay or award increases for protest groups such as pensioners or trade unions.

ARTICLE 9 RATIONALE-: The Police service appears to require redeployment & reduction of Red Tape which destroys police moral. Notes & paperwork, which are probabally the cause of most of the frustration in the service, but maybe essential for accountability. However, such notes might be substituted by miniture magnetic tape recorders capable of being downloaded onto computers & of being formalised by civilian employees. The redeployment might best be brought about by careful implementation of New York's ex Police Chief Bill Bretton's successful methods which utilised Compstat computer technology plus Bobbies on the beat...a combined strategy which the US Police Chief thinks more important than throwing taxpayers cash at the problem of runaway crime on the streets. There is a need for change of political & operational attitude re public reaction to criminal activity where the 'have a go Jo ' is liable to be arrested. This may lead to the Public lending a hand when an outnumbered Policeman or a fellow citizen is attacked by thugs.

Personal experience of police complaint proceedure indicates that it can be biased. The police did not proceed with a personal case involving criminal damage. Due to the lack of lawful power, the 'trouble' resulted in some three more years of un-necessary misery. After settling matters with a Court Order, which cost the other party about £10,000, the Police complaint proceedure was invoked. But the investigating officer walking smartly away after 'misinterpreting' my remarks about 'not wishing to kick coppers ankles' before I could add 'but I want to see justice done'.. It is believed this was, in part, because the other party had a relative who held the rank of a senior police officer.

However, a report in Luton & Dunstable on Sunday dated 16th April 2002 suggests that Anti Social Behaviour Orders can turn around some teenagers from hell. But the problem maybe so far out of hand that the re-introduction of the birch may be needed to provide an effective deterent. Talking to people at random indicates that there is widespread support from 'the man in the street' for the return of Corporal Punishment. This matter should be put to a referendum to settle the matter....since the abandonment of this successful deterent has seen an enormous rise in cost due to mass employment of 'N' Social Workers & Probation Officers.... a policy which has not achieved the desired effect but has somehow successfully transferred sympathy from victim to the thug. Increasing the strokes of the birch from one for a repeat offence to a max of five for the sixth offence would weed out 99% of present day repeat offenders...leaving long term jail space for the remainder of 'hard case offenders'. Such a policy would also help to reduce the need for more prison capacity!
-

- ARTICLE 9 CLAUSE 27 requires that the recommendations of ex NY Police Chief B Bretton's methods of Bobbies on the beat plus the employment of Compstat computer technology & minature voice &, if possible, video cameras/recorders be given a trial run with the objective of improving Police efficiency, detection rates & morale.

-

- CLAUSE 28 requires public debate & a referendum to decide whether or not to the restore Corporal Punishmen for repeat violent offences as outlined in ARTICLE 9 Rationale. CLAUSE 29 requires the Police complaint proceedure is conducted before an independant tribunal.

-

ARTICLE 10 Rationale-: Residential street tidiness needs some attention particularly when caused by residents from other streets. Many of these non residents park personal & company owned trucks, vans & salesmans vehicles overnight. Others dump long term, eg holiday periods, vehicles suffering mechanical breakdown. Frequently these vehicles are filthy, drive over & damage mowed verges & or leak oil. In some cases the vehicles obstruct vision therefore posing a hazard. The often battered, dirty & broken down vehicles are a depressing sight & discourage residential pride, a factor that leaves fences unrepaired & or unpainted....leading to further dedcline in standards. The 'down grading' escalates to litter being deposited on the road....& ultimately encourages teenage vandalism to the bordering properties. The Council, Councillors & police, when they can be cornered claim they can do nothing. Limiting the time permitted for 'on street parking' to four hours might be one answer....but the authorities tend to talk about the costly need of patrols to establish the enforcement. But it is thought co-operative action from police when alerted by concerned residents would economically put an end to such problems. The Police are also reported as preferring non resident parking where it avoids obstructing 'through' roads...but they do not have to suffer the unacceptable results of their supporting action. It is also pointed out many offenders have a garage, possibly filled with junk ! Cul de Sacs are paid for & built for the convenience of house owners who reside in the said Cul de Sac & the point needs to be recognised!

- ARTICLE 10 CLAUSE 30-:It is a requirement of CLAUSE 30 that enforcable parking limits are imposed when requested by a majority of cul- de sacs' residents.

- CLAUSE 31 requires that LA take litter bugs to Court where witnesses or photographic evidence is available. Convicted offenders would face heavy fines.

- CLAUSE 32 requires that persistantly untidy neighbours be dealt with in a similar way to 'litter bugs' in CLAUSE 31.

ARTICLE 11 RATIONALE-:The responsibility for Owner Occupiers' relief from tree problems is dealt within ARTICLE 2 of this document. Matters such as irresponsible bird feeding problems, for example, may need similar attention. In itself, bird feeding is harmless...except, perhaps, to birds themself. But as with every harmless activity there are people who, for one reason or another still cause a nuisense to their neighbours.

For example, irresponsible over feeding can cause food to be left out 24 hours, 7 days. This causes locally increased artificial bird population levels, rat infestations & is a danger to public health. Depending on the size of the garden & its surroundings the 'landing approach' feeding birds employ can also cause a nuisense to neighbours....especially when quantities of food cause a 'frenzied' feed mode to occur. It is then that the large species of birds appear such as messy seagulls, pigeons etc...which increases & speeds the process of messing up washing put out to dry/fencing/paintwork & brickwork. Neighbours who impinge their excesses over their boundaries are out of order. These & like matters should be dealt with in the small claims court [see ARTICLE 12] as a private matter since the LA 's often fail to act!.

- ARTICLE 11 CLAUSE 33 gives an Owner Occupier/Householder who suffer a nuisense, say from careless bird feeding neighbours [or other nuisanses, see ARTICLE 12] to have a near automatic right to request the Court to impose an inforcement order on the perpetuator of the nuisense. Councils have now have a right to impose an ASBO but some Councils/Cllrs refuse to implement the ordres! And that henceforth, use of a bird feeding dispensers that precludes big birds & rats involvement are manditory & exclusive of other feeding methods in densely

- populated areas.

- CLAUSE 34 grants the public similar rights over noise abatement since Council Noise Abatement actions can be inadequate where Housing Associations or Asylum Seekers are involved, when, for example, a claim of 'racism' freezes action where immigrants are involved. Noise measuring equiptment will be made available for rental from the local library.

- CLAUSE 35 grants the public the right to pursue other nuisense problems in a a no nonsense Court action & a full bi-annually updated list of admissable complaints would be updated in the Small Claims Court. [See ARTICLE 12]

ARTICLE 12 RATIONALE-: Citizens seeking relief from listed nuisenses [apply to Small Claim Court for updated versions of admissable comlaints] will be entitled to cheap , informal no nonsense relief from said nuisenses by means of a Court Order to be executed within a reasonable & specified time limit. Failure of the offender to grant specified relief within given time limit would render the judgement liable to County Court action for automatic imposing of ongoing penal fines until the offended complies with Court Order or is bankrupted. It is thought that most cases of nuisanse would then be settled over the garden fence by mutual agreement.

- ARTICLE 12 CLAUSE 36 grants a citizen seeking relief from the said 'listed nuisenses' [or the update list held in the Small Claims Court] shall be granted a low cost near automatic judgement in the form of a small claims Court Order conferring relief within a stated time limit. Failure to comply with such a Court Order, or its time limit, would then give the agrieved party the right to a no nonsense County Court Order imposing a non- complience daily fine until complience or bankruptcy occurs. The default payment would include the defaulter's property, if necessary.

- CLAUSE 37 tasks MPs , LA & CC Councillors to update the Home Office with commonly met nuisenses [such as non residents enjoying long term parking facilities in Cul de Sacs] who would bi-annually update the Small Claims Nuisense lists.

ARTICLE 13 RATIONALE -: An alternative to much debated proportional representition that will remedy the problem of excess/inadequate parliamentary majority is presented which, it is thought can limit an 'elbowing' PMs ability to easily override Parliament & or enable backbenchers to differntiate between useless & hamstrung PMs is herewith proposed in CLAUSE 38.

- ARTICLE 13 CLAUSE 38 requires the difference between the total number of Parliamentary Opposition Voters & the Parliamentary Government Voters to be reduced/ increased to a number to be agreed by an all Parties Committee by allocating a less than or greater than one vote value to each member. For the purposes of example, a number of thirty majority votes is suggested.

- CLAUSE 3 to be added to /updated /amended or completed as information permits.

- DC Tissington dated Janurary 2007
cc PM, Mr D Cameron MP Ldr Opp, Mr D Davies MP S Home Sec, Mr C Kennedy MP, Mr C Chope, MP OBE, Ms M Moran, ADCI P Whatmore, Fraud Squad, Mr P Hill, Express, Mr J Bryant D Mail, ED Dunstable on Sunday, ED Luton Gazette, BBC Three Counties Radio
See writers 'OBSERVATIONS ON G8 SUMMIT 2005' dated August 2005
**See Classical Environmental Folly Ed 5

REF 6

3

Table 1 also shows for each tree species the distance between tree and building within which 75 per cent and 90 per cent of the cases of damage occurred. It shows that some species of tree present a greater risk than others to building foundations. In particular, oaks lead the table by some way; this is consistent with

BRE experience, which indicates that the extent and depth of drying around oak trees can be significantly greater than occurs with most other species. However, it is important to remember that, in addition to the variations in behaviour *between* species, there are significant variations *within* species.

Table 1 Risk of damage by different tree species

Species	Max tree height H in metres	Max distance in metres for 75% of cases	Max distance in metres for 90% of cases
Oak	16 – 23	13	18
Poplar	24	15	20
Ash	23	10	13
Elm*	20 – 25	12	19
False acacia	18 – 20	8.5	10.5
Horse chestnut	16 – 25	10	15
Hawthorn	10	7	8.7
Lime	16 – 24	8	11
Willow	15	11	18
Beech	20	9	11
Plane	25 – 30	7.5	10
Apple, Pear	8 – 12	6	8
Sycamore, Maples	17 – 24	9	12
Cherries, Plums, Damsons, etc	6 – 12	6	7.5
Birch	12 – 14	7	8
Cypresses, Cupressus	18 – 25	3.5	5
Rowan, Service tree	8 – 12	7	8.5

* Ranking obtained by assuming a planting frequency of 1%

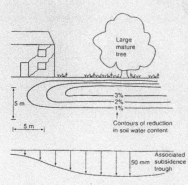

Damage to buildings

Damage to a building results from distortions of the building (Digest 251), not simply from foundation movement. Therefore, the lateral distribution of movements associated with trees and clay soils are important. Figure 2 illustrates how a large mature tree can affect soil water contents laterally, together with the profile of subsidence that might accompany such changes in water content. It is the variations in foundation movement that have caused the damage to the building, not the absolute movement.

Figure 2 Lateral variation of soil water content and associated subsidence profile

REF 7

This could all come true if we

<u>WITHDREW</u>

from the EU

WE WILL KEEP OUR POUND
No Euro

WE WILL ONCE AGAIN HAVE A SAY
Decision making at Westminster

OUR COURTS WILL NOT BE SUBJECTED
TO FOREIGN LAW

WE WILL REGAIN OUR
FISHING GROUNDS FOR OUR
FISHERMEN

WE WILL SET OUR OWN
AGRICULTURAL POLICY
*and offer our farmers the help
they need.*

WE WILL RETAIN CONTROL OVER OUR
ARMED FORCES

WE WILL REMOVE THE 'RED TAPE' THAT
IS STRANGLING OUR BUSINESSES

WE WILL KEEP OUR OIL,
GAS AND GOLD RESERVES

WE WILL SAVE OVER £1 MILLION POUNDS
EVERY HOUR, DAY AND NIGHT!

ONLY THE UNITED KINGDOM
INDEPENDENCE PARTY
INSISTS THAT WE MUST

WITHDRAW

FROM THE EUROPEAN UNION,
RENEGOTIATE OUR TRADE TERMS
AND KEEP OUR POUND FOR EVER.

*All the other parties, despite their
slogans, are committed to "Full British
Membership Of The European Union"*

UNITED KINGDOM
INDEPENDENCE
PARTY

PROSPERITY AND FREE TRADE
OUTSIDE THE EU

The South West Regional Office, PO Box 1714 Salisbury, SP1 2UQ
Tel: 01722 411 313. Fax: 01722 413 025
E-mail: independence@btinternet.com

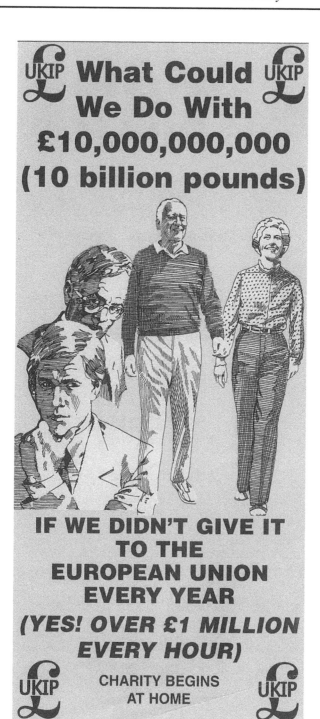

WITH £10 BILLION

We will have the nurses we need

We will have more 'Bobbies' on the beat

We will help our farmers and fishermen

We will rebuild our armed forces

'CHARITY BEGINS AT HOME'

Membership Application

If you believe that we should be a free country with our own government and our own laws trading in a world market and managing our own finances and pensions, please join us in the fight against being just a European Region.

The UKIP is a non sectarian, non racist body with no prejudices against foreigners or lawful minorities of any kind.

I would like to become a member of the
UNITED KINGDOM INDEPENDENCE PARTY   ☐

I WOULD LIKE MORE INFORMATION   ☐

Please ✓one box

Surname ....

Forenames ....

Address ....

....

....

.... .Post Code ....

Telephone. .... Date ....

Subscriptions:- Annual fee £15
OAPs/Students/Benefit Recipients £7

Signed ....

Please send this form with subscription
(and donation if you wish) to:

UKIP South West Region,
PO Box 1714 Salisbury, SP1 2UQ
Tel: 01722 411 313

County Contacts

Bristol 0117 962 9761
Cornwall 01736 360 607
Devon 01803 557 433
Dorset 01258 880 808
Gloucestershire 01451 850 778
Somerset 01984 656 313
Wiltshire 01380 830 264

REF 8

A REPORT REQUESTING PARLIAMENT FOR COUNCIL TAX REDUCTION

INTRODUCTION

This report has been produced to provide rationale, in conjunction
with Figures 1 and 2, for phased reduction of a residential or
council tax for years 1999, 2000 through to 2005. Said Tax was
initiated in 1993 to replace the reviled poll tax. The poll tax was
introduced in 1989 in order to bring more taxpayers to fund council
activities since the rates, which the poll tax replaced, put the onus
of council funding on, among others, the principal occupier of a
residential property. Many people think the poll tax should have been
retained but this tax failed for two main reasons....namely the non
householder occupiers of a property often moved from one dwelling to
another making collection of the tax expensive or even impossible. The
second reason for this particular levy failure was excessive demand
per capita. [see peak demand figure 2, 1990 & trough 1992 which was
funded by 2.5% increase in VAT that we think ought now to be reduced
to 15%!] Although the data used in this report is derived from the
record over the on going lifetime of a 1959 Dorset based D band
property, the explication is thought generally to apply to most Local
Authorities, Nationwide.

It seems that the local and county authorities may have lost sight
of the purpose for which they were evolved. This was to provide
essential services for local householders, local businesses and
companies at a competitive cost. A little thought will show from
first principles that a residential property should not be utilised as
a tax extraction tool... since the occupier needs the facility in
order to survive. This is generally recognised by HM Treasury which
allows tax free sale of ones main house or residence and although
householders can make profit from such activities, any gain is
usually much less than it appears to be because of inflation,
mortgage, maintenance, removal and `next property' costs.

Minimum cost regarding LAs services is obviously necessary from the
occupiers point of view whether they be newly weds, family raisers or
pensioners in order to more easily over-ride periods of financial
difficulty, eg redundancy, illness or infirmity. In the limit, these
hardships, when added to excessive local taxes, may be the last straw
causing repossession of mortgaged property and marriage breakup.

However, the requirements do not end there. Local Authorities,
indeed all governments and their agencies, [including Brussels] are
overheads. It is obvious, although frequently overlooked, that
overheads must be minimised to make any Corporation viable... ask any
businessman.... and that goes for UK Co Ltd: too. The latter reason
given for requirement of lower costs is obviously in the National
interest when one realises that in 84/85, LAs spent some 25% of GNP
and employed about 14% of the Nation`s work force. [Source Department
of Environment Leaflet, 1986.ENV1 JO120N] However, LAs have now
sufficiently increased their financial demands to seriously upset both
domestic and national budgets. They are , of consequence, mainly, or
in part, responsible for Bank of England currently imposed high
interest rates which so besets mortgage payers and the business
community. That is, LAs have caused significant wage demands from the
nations`s work force to fund council activities, thereby increasing
the cost of manufactured goods and services. This increase in
overheads is obviously not helpful to a nation that lives by exporting

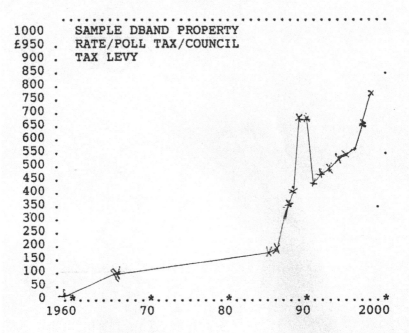

FIGURE 1

PAGE 3 of 17

DATE	DCC EX £M GROSS	NET	CBC EX £M GROSS	NET	EX £M POLICE	SAMPLE D BAND RATES/PT/CT	PROP'Y LEVY £ SEWAGE	WATER
59/60						25.2	INCL	2.8
67						110	NK	NK
85	254	189.1	7.9	1.18	31.5	172	NK	13
86	277	212.2	5.9	1.9	32.5	189	41	20
87	302	229.4	6.4	2.1	35.5	377	66	25
88	333	250	6.85	2.1	NG	407	74	26
89	356	274.6	8.4	2.7	NG	678	80	30
90	384	305	14.9	2.5	47.2	678	87	35
91	439	335.8	13.1	2.6	52.8	430	98	41
92	484	369	13.6	3.02	59.4	480	106	47
93	481	357.5	13.9	3.10	60.7	491	116	57
94	502	373.9	14.54	3.65	64.6	524	123	59
95	454	358	15.3	3.4	67.5	537	128	70
96	475	379	15.69	3.58	68.1	567	133	80
97	285	225.5	16.6	3.81	74	665	141	83
98	294	238.8	16.7	3.86	77.4	759	151	87

NB Borough Council records show earliest valuation of sample D Band property in 1959 as £28. Sales Brochure for same property show general rates as 18 shillings [£0.9] & water rate as 2 shillings [£0.1] in the pound!

% increase in rates/poll tax/council tax from 1959 to 1998 = 3011%

% increase in RATES/PT/CT tax + SEWAGE from 1959 to 1998 = 3611%

% increase in RPI [ALL ITEMS] from 1959 to 1998 = 551%

Police independently funded from 1995 onward.

1991/92 Poll Tax reduction achieved by government intervention aided by increase of VAT by 2.5%

CC & BC started progressive Manpower reductions in 1995/96 &1993/94 res:

FIGURE 2
----

finished goods! If the manufacturer tries to cover the extra costs by increased production, always assuming such extra goods can be sold, then the already over plundered earth gets an even bigger demand placed on its finite resources. Environmentalists please note!

It is necessary to point out that one cannot attach all of the blame for continued escalating cost/taxes to LA/County Councillors even though they do not appear to heed appeals for council tax restraint. Indeed, some councillors state the need to preserve tradition takes preference to CT reduction!

One should also bear in mind the HUGE National load of Revenue Services Benefits which amounts to financial support of housing costs and Council Tax to low income households. This benefit is, in part, self inflicted by Council`s non stop increased council tax demand which transcends the inflation rate. Said financial support maybe compared to a two wheeled scout hand cart with manhandling shafts each end of the conveyance. Scout A lifts the shafts at end A of the cart. Scout B opposes the `self inflicted' load by providing extra lift at end B. If sufficient `lift' is available the wheels of the cart leave the ground....which is what tends to happen to the said Council Tax support when the LA tax demand escalates; as it has done. Using the eight LAs in Dorset as an example, it can be seen that the national financial load is a serious matter which amounts to about a £1 billion [plus circulatory losses around IR/ Treasury which may bring totals to £1.5B]. The said amount acts as an hidden addition to said CT!

However, Whitehall and its Quangos /Agencies often compel extra tasks on county/local government... sometimes without regard to practicability or sufficient financial consideration. Remember too, that local funding from national government suffers a bigger loss on its journey from our other pocket via the Treasury to the LA, ie, it is an inefficient act. Likewise, Brussels frequently treats Whitehall in a similar manner... and the financial losses on any grants received en route to where so ever are even larger! It is thought these matters need addressing by MPs and, without regard to sacred cows, in order that reasonable local & national financial controls are exercised in the UK. The writer, who has collected some 7000 signatures in support of the aim to reduce council tax, aims to start matters off by delivering the petition and this completed report to 10 Downing Street for the attention of the Prime Minister.

HOW BRUSSELS AFFECTS LOCAL SPENDING

Europe or Brussels has intervened in GBs national & local affairs [hence its place in this report], and mostly to our detriment, to an ever increasing level. The encroachment by Brussels, which affects local & national expenditure, has been drip fed to the British Public by successive Parliaments. The public express their disapproval as best they can in the national papers, J. Young Radio 2 Polls and in informal discussion throughout the land. It is perhaps time our politicians, who represent us, really called a halt. Either the EU PROPERLY mends its ways by re-writing the various Treaties; or GB must restate and re-negotiate its position whilst insisting on its rights to trade with Europe under the terms of the Treaty of Rome.

The ongoing blackmail is put into perspective when one realises that Europe & GB have a mutual need of each other's trade. In the event, our European cousins might show continued hostility but they could hardly ACT with more hostility than they already have to date! We, the British people have given the Europeans their freedom over the centuries at great cost in terms of blood and money. It may now be time for a reversal.

However, Parliament tends to view each problem from separate water-tight compartments. With hind sight, so called solutions to the multitude of problems that confront us today have replaced traditional methods... resulting in costly failures. As such, problems appear to be inadequately dealt with and lead to the glorious mix up this report is exposing. As least, we need to `back track' and maybe reform the very structure of Ministries, and of, consequence Parliament itself; not least because the local & national muddle appears to stem from `growing like Topsy'. That is, unless one subscribes to the theory that the `Brotherhood' of International, National & Locally linked bureaucrats `cement' each other's jobs together by intertwining `separately' linked legislation! The following observations reveal or highlight part of the mostly undesirable impact Brussels has had on our local activities & financial affairs.

It has recently been announced that run down housing communities from the public sector are to be uplifted to the tune of some £800 million, a local expenditure committed by UK National Government. One maybe hard pressed to fault the sentiment. But TV newscasts pictured the PM against the backdrop of run down property suffering the effects of graffiti and vandalised windows boarded up [which tends to indicate solutions stemming from repeated damage.] This sort of damage usually emanates from the action of undisciplined children who show little regard for surrounding property or people. Remonstration often ends in the protester being beaten up or even stabbed. The parents are frequently seen defending such thuggery and smirking at the inability of the law to bring such behaviour to a grinding halt. There is need to HARSHLY penalise parents who support such conduct.

It is here that Brussel's non-elected officials add to the problem by wrongly forbidding responsible parents [and schoolteachers] the use of a cane. These officials should be removed from all input or control of UK law by what ever means necessary. The writer [and his children] were disciplined with the proper use of a cane both at home and at school. The cane clearly has a beneficial effect on some children as they approach ten years of age when the parent often find a hand smack inadequate or that access to a running child hard to deal with without a cane. In any event, not a penny of public money should be spent on renovation of said houses until the afore mentioned shortcomings have been PROPERLY dealt with.

My extensive dealings with the public lead me to believe the public want thugs outside the age of parental control to be dealt with by use of the birch plus Military Glass House treatment where movement is carried out on the trot... irrespective of the views of Brussels. The argument about miscarriage of justice and the finality of capital punishment is accepted; but before we hear misdirected murmurings of brutality re: the request for introduction of corporal punishment etc, let the murmurer direct his hat in the correct direction. That is, to give sympathy to the injured pensioner, abused child, raped, mugged, stabbed citizen/hospital worker and direct corporal punishment at the thug. Sliding scale doses of the penalties suggested for repeated offence would quickly reduce thuggery, make life more tolerable for the citizen and THE TAXPAYER since probationary officers, closed circuit TV surveillance aids, their shift manning requirements & prison services would no longer enter the equation to the same degree; if at all. It should be noted that CCTV is rendered much less than effective unless there is 100% coverage ...which is impracticable on grounds of overall costs. And before the foregoing is dismissed, it is thought government should put the matters raised to a referendum. It ought then implement the findings without further ado.

However, matters do not end here. There is the matter of open boarder policy...another Brussel inspired nonsense. We in GB now end up being invaded and accepting all or most of the economic destitutes of Europe and elsewhere. LAs have to house these unfortunate `refuges and the local taxpayer foot this bill plus the Social Security costs from his/her other pocket! Our political masters should consider reducing the manpower at the Home Office, [who state they are too short of funds to deal with illegal immigrants] thus releasing funds to tighten boarder controls, speed up repatriation policy by means of instant turnaround... with or without the agreement of our non-elected task-masters at Brussels!. All in all, GB must be amusing the rest of Europe to tolerate the foregoing never mind ALL the other ruinous games played on us by our European cousins...eg CAP & what appears to be industrial sabotage! We are not so much being governed, we are being systematically stripped of all we have fought and worked for by all and sundry.

HOW WHITEHALL AFFECTS LOCAL SPENDING

One of the main ways in which Whitehall questionably affects local spending is through its agents, eg English Heritage etc plus The Town & Country Planning Acts. There is nothing fundamentally wrong with protecting Listed Buildings, provided they are not residential dwellings. But the requirement should not be funded in any way by local taxpayers through Council Tax. There is doubt if the sine qua non should be funded by the national tax payer either. Monuments and like structures are of some importance but the management & contributions for upkeep should be from National Lottery, admission ticket sales & voluntary subscriptions only. Expensive whims such as tunnelling under Stonehenge & Tower of London are best described as spending good taxpayers and or lottery money in a frivolous manner. Such acts also indicate a lack of respect for the rules of commerce which dictate that overheads be minimised. If it were just Stonehenge [should the need arises there are plenty of equally old replacement stones in Wales] one might turn a blind eye. But the scope of extravagance beggars belief! The complete amount of work that has been `ordered' by English Heritage is unknown but their influence to `compel' expenditure [believed derived from T&CPActs] extends to many cathedrals, steeples, castles, bridges, water/windmills and large residential country mansions.

Restoration work is made additionally expensive, eg, by petty arguments about the exact proportions of various ingredients of mortar in order to produce the colour that matches `experts` imagination. Other expensive areas include archeology. The Times, May 18` 94 reports the 1st phase of English Heritage recovery of a single left tibia from a Sussex gravel pit. It cost 0.75M to `find`.. The second phase, with no further discovery, if my memory serve me well, took the final cost to £2M. Expensive `post mortems` and reconstruction of face tissue conducted on collections of old bones utilising computer enhanced face recreation techniques are also `the order of the day'. All in all, especially in view of property repossessions and business failures, it is thought that the local/national tax payer & his/her assets are not treated with proper respect by the powers that be. The Times, 15th May `94 states Hi Tech spending to the tune of £4 Billion failed to cut the number of Whitehall Staff, a feat which contrasts with British Telecom who reduced staffing levels from 250000 to 150000 after the 1981 privatisation scheme!

Daniel Tissington

LOCAL & COUNTY COUNCIL BUDGETS

The following text is not aimed at any particular council, although
the records providing the data are mainly derived from Dorset based
Authorities demands or information literature. The observations are
generally thought to apply nationwide because of similarities of
records/memories obtained when the writer's residence was situated in
Hertfordshire, newspaper reports and discussions held with neighbours
and members of the public enjoying vacations in Dorset.

Perhaps a broad-based deduction, which may form a good base line, is
the best place to begin. It seems there maybe general moves within
Whitehall, Local Authorities , including County, to hive off the more
essential services, eg sewage &, in some cases, water...services
which were made fully independent a decade or so ago. Another facility
which has issued its own budget since 1995, but whose funding is still
collected by the local council, is the Police Force. Furthermore, it
is believed consideration is now being given to separate the
financing of rubbish /recycling services. And, it is thought that the
fire service may well follow these examples by eventually issuing
their own budget.

Whereas there maybe advantage in the rescheduling of funding
arrangements described in the above paragraph, there is a serious
downside to semi independent or completely independent funding
arrangements. A service that is made partially or fully independent of
L & or CC for its funding continues to escalate [some think grossly]
its charges. However, the local council & county council also
continue to escalate their expenditures and, as far as can be seen,
without proper remission for discharged responsibilities. Of
consequence, the council tax demands continue to increases as before
the changeover occurred. [see figure 2 for detail of Water, Sewage &
Local taxes charge] That is, whether it was planned or not, the public
seem to have been set up for increased financial outgoing /taxation.
The same possibility exists re: other services!. Furthermore, some of
the County/LA's escalating proportion of this extra tax appear to be
applied in increased amounts to what are thought to be non-essentials,
ie in areas which should have no influence on taxes & charges made
against a primary necessity of survival; such as a home. It is clear
that this form of financial wizardry should not be allowed to escalate
into complete or partial independence of council funding regarding the
police, recycling & fire services.... without safeguards being in
place to protect the local & national taxpayer from double charging
or unnecessary new charges. Particular examples of the foregoing are
given -:

As stated, the DCC 1995 & ongoing budgets no longer fund Dorset
Police Authority. By referring to the DCC `94 budget, it can be
deduced that the omission of said expense would reduce the DCC
liability by some £64.6M. However, as far as can be seen, the `95 DCC
Net Expenditure [total cost of annual projects less grants , ticket
sales etc.] was only reduced by £15.6M. Admittedly, Nat: Gov: `95
Specific Grants to DCC were reduced by £37M...but the DPA received
£38.5M in grants in `95...so lets not blame reduced grants for extra
DCC spending on this occasion! And remember the taxpayer still had to
part fund the DPA via CBC funding. 1995 DCC literature seem to
indicate that £41.7M extra was spent on routine services. This extra
expenditure was reduced by introducing £11.1M credit...of which £10.9M
was found from Asset Management Reserve Account [AMRA] WHICH HAD NOT
HITHERTO BEEN MENTIONED IN DCC TAXPAYER ISSUED LITERATURE. It promptly

raises the question -: Where did this £10.9M come from?... answer preferably in greater detail than `from the taxpayers pockets' please. It also produces more puzzling questions-:

1] Why was so much extra cash raised in `95 by DCC from the hard pressed taxpayer in the first place? ...ie did the `95 income help to fund the AMRA?
2] Did this `95 DCC Budget produce `an over elevated base line' upon which to set even higher DCC `96 budget?
3] Whilst accepting that some reserves are necessary, the CBC admit, in `95 to reserves of at least £13.4M. Documents issued to the public from DCC & DORSET POLICE AUTH: do not state the amounts supporting their fund/s. However, The DPA`s AMRA has provided more than £7.6M for years `95/99 toward costs. How much tax payers money is tied up in these various Authorities Multi-Numbered Reserves?

In 1991, CBC Housing stock was sold to Twynham Housing Association. According to the local press, [New Milton Times 23rd Feb `91] & unlike New Forest District Council [NFDC], CBC did not reveal the sum agreed for the transfer of the housing stock. Perhaps this secrecy is because CBC claim [incorrectly it is thought, see 1990/`91 transfer from Housing Revenue Account of £.022150M to general fund, &, Revenue Services Benefits] that the local taxpayer has never been affected by the council house finances. Whatever the facts of the matter, it is thought the LAs should account for ALL debits and credits.

SAMPLES AREAS OF CBC BUDGET WITH POSSIBILITY FOR FINANCIAL CUTBACK

CBC`s Estimated Departmental Budgets for 1998/`99 -:
Finance & Gen: Purposes Committee bal: to summary -: £1237070
Leisure   "   "   "   "   "   £1315590
Planning & Environment   "   "   "   "   "   £1216720
Policy & Resources   "   "   "   "   "   £1000580
Technical Services   "   "   "   "   "   £1141110

The following budget data supplied by CBC give insight of rationale
behind the intended blanket type statements in RECOMMENDATIONS-1-2 &
3 suggesting possibility of Local/County Council expenditure cuts.

CBC Finance & General Purposes Committee-:
The 1998/`99 CBC Estimated Budget for Mayoral charges are   £81990 per
year, inclusive of running the Mayor`s Parlour. [a listed building
with more than one function claimed] A Local Newspaper report in Jan
1992 quotes New Forest District Council`s Mayoral costs as £12000 per
year versus CBC`s then £78000!! .

Revenue Services Benefits provide support to housing costs & Council
Tax to low income households. 1998/`99 Expenditure £7,910,340. [£7.9
MILLION+] Income [presumably Government Grants] £7,387,260. Bal
carried to summary £523080. SEE PARA 5, INTRODUCTION FOR `SELF
INFLICTED' reasoning.

CBC 1998/`99 Leisure Committee Expenditure & Capital Charges on Regent
Centre £0.104710M ; Income £0.001900M.

Regent Centre restoration declared a priority. Estimate of cost given
as £0.668M. [See Christchurch Advertiser Oct 8th `98] .

RECREATION GROUNDS CF to summary after deducting income of £.062M is
£596590 mainly to maintenance of open spaces, accessible to the
public, offering recreational/environmental needs consisting of trees,
formal floral beds etc.

PLANNING COMMITTEE
See RECOMMENDATIONS 1, 2 & Appendix.

POLICIES & RESOURCES COMMITTEE For year 1998/`99 £0.429M went to
Highcliffe Castle of which an unstated proportion is funded by English
Heritage/National Lottery. No income is reported! Added to this, over
the years, are newspaper reports of other substantial amounts of cash
poured into Highcliffe Castle...but one really has no idea whether
these reported proposals are carried or dropped.

CBC are known to own at least FIVE Listed Buildings and, possibly,
two bridges at Christchurch. The cost of renovating & maintaining
these & other buildings is not known with precision. However, at the
Consultation Meeting dated 09 February,98 where the Budget for `98/99
was reviewed by representatives of Non Domestic Ratepayers & Council
Tax Payers it was verbally stated that some twenty years earlier £1M
[apart from ongoing yearly charges plus] was borrowed to fund work to
CBC Highcliffe Castle. The loan, which has not been repaid, was said
to have attracted a another £1M total & ongoing interest.

Place Mill restoration was declared complete in June `91. Cost
estimated by writer, bearing in mind Mills are more complicated than

buildings which are static items, around £1M. [Writer unable to confirm costs] [1998/`99 Expenditure & Capital Charges on said Mill £0.019320M; Income£0.008400M.

CBC Policies & Resources Committee list five CBC Corporate Properties let on full commercial rent. 1998/`99 Expenditure & Capital Charges on said properties is £.1926M, income is £.068M

TECHNICAL SERVICES COMMITTEE
Technical Staff & Overheads claim an Ex & Income of £.792370 M

Departmental Administration claim an Ex & Income of £.480460 M

Tech: Staff & Overheads claim an Ex & Income of £.792370 M

The sum total of the above three entries totals £2,065200 M but is not carried to summary.

CCTV 1998/`99 expenditure /capital charges £141000 against £83120 for year 1997/`98. [+168%]

Radio Mast & Equipment Expenditure Capital Charges £0.022210M. Income [presumably from private commercial firms] £0.019750.

SAMPLE AREAS OF DCC BUDGET WITH POSSIBILITIES FOR FINANCIAL CUTBACK
The DCC net expenditure [gross figure less grants, fees charges] for 1998/`99 is £238.8M. The expenditure percentage is -:

ITEM		%
1	Employees	48%
2	Premises	05%
3	Transport	04%
4	Supplies & Services	07%
5	Highways Maint:	03%
6	Student Awards/Comm: Care/3rd Parties	25%
7	Cap Financing	08%

The sparse information available makes firm proposals for cutback difficult. However, the writer has given suggestions which may apply to items [1]-[6] These prospects will be given in RECOMMENDATIONS 3.

RECOMMENDATIONS 1   GENERAL

In keeping with the aims & findings of the foregoing text it is very evident that Governments, International, National, County or Local should operate utility services only on taxpayer money. They should not indulge in business or businesses of any sort because risk taking requires particular expertise, which may or may not be applied. Additionally, he who pays the piper....ie financing risk taking should be the prerogative of the financier. In capitalised ventures where money is put up for Services/ Company Shares or legally binding agreed profit & loss sharing schemes; the proposed 'use' dividing line of money derived from taxation and from voluntary means is obviously needed. It is fair and clear cut.

Governments, International, National, County or Local should not manage or own Listed Buildings, Buildings, Land or Structures of any sort with the exception of Buildings or Land that provide Storage Facilities for Service Materials or Offices for Administration of Utility Services to the Local Council Tax paying Public.

RECOMMENDATIONS 2

The expenditure of Leisure Committee of £0.545810M on recreation grounds seems excessive when one considers that the Christchurch Borough only contains about 20000 hereditaments.

It is thought CBC would be more cost effectively served by mobile telephones rather than the Radiomast. One notices that all the privately run maintenance builders in the area are now so equipped these days...so presumably it is cost effective & rental rates currently achieved by CBC will, presumably, decline.

Coastal protection work is costly & maybe, with the melting of the ice caps DUE TO EXCESSIVE POPULATION LEVELS, a waste of money. The rising sea levels will generally erode the soft coast line until it reaches rock. King Canute, who had no 'green house gas problems' knew better!

Town Twinning costs are not known & it is thought these costs have no bearing on essential LA work.

Planning Services currently levy a charge for some of their services. It is not sure when this practise was introduced...but it would appear to be a form of double charging for a Council Service which is a legal requirement. It is felt that the T&CPAs should be re written as in its present form the rights of both Parties are not clear. The said ambiguity makes for expensive [Court Cases/Inquiries] and difficult administration on the one hand with frustration, delay & expense on the other hand. It may also contribute to the concentration of too much arbitrary power in the hands of the LA. See expansion in APPENDIX, attached.

Techinical Services £2.0652M [not carried to summary] is, presumably, received from other CBC or DCC Departments. It is a large sum of money for the taxpayer to find & it is thought the accounts are insufficiently detailed to pass proper judgement.

RECOMMENDATIONS 3

DCC biggest commitment, 48% of net expenditure, is to employees. This obviously applies to Dorset C C Staff, Fire Service, Teachers etc. many of whom claim to be special cases. Whereas it is not suggested that Staff should be short changed it has to be said that a job is only available if someone is prepared to pay for the service provided. Around each autumn, the same old cry is heard from County Hall & the LA that Council Taxes will rise significantly due to wage/pension [see Christchurch Advertiser 1st Oct `98/Sunday Times 29th March `98] requirements of the various public facilities. It is human nature for employees to think they are a special case. [we all do including us unemployed pensioners] but money has to be earned. You cannot print it....without suffering the consequences! Large `catch up settlements' fairly recently awarded to Firemen, Policemen, etc. are soon forgotten & `repeats' become the order of the day! It maybe Councillors & Council Officials, do not enjoy the normal authoritarian relationship between paymaster & employee personnel. That is, the whole relationship between the parties is too impersonal & Councils may not be best equipped to deal with such problems. It is possible that the whole business should be transferred to a management team or carefully contracted out to a commercial organisation & funded from Whitehall.

If the above recommendation is adopted...it maybe County Hall or Halls could be sold off.

In any event, it seems to me that a leaf might also be taken from Hants CC who are re-organising the Fire Service by reciting the Fire Stations. It is thought that surviving Fire Service Units might be better able to accommodate any reduction in their numbers by making use of purpose equipped trucks or even `deluxe Green Goddesses' complete with ladder and hoses. This auxiliary equipment could be economically housed in locally custom built garages & manned by local part timers equipped with mobile phones.. The part time situations could be used as stepping stones to permanent positions at a Main Fire Station [thereby providing part timers with incentive to perform well] & such units could `hold the fort' until the strategically located main equipment arrived.

And finally, the figure of 25% of a net budget totalling some 238M awarded to Students, Community Care & Third Parties appears excessive.

NB 1990 DCC payments to Students were just 6% of net spending.

APPENDIX
The following is mainly an amended abstract from Edition 5,
Classical Environmental Folly, [1992]. [Lodged in major UK Ref:
Libraries]

Much of the UK & other nation's planning laws seem to fail to stand
up to investigation for fundamental reasons. As with Conservation &
Tree Preservation Orders [CO & TPOs are part of the UK T&CPAs] the
T&CPAs concept seems to embrace the Creed of Communism, that is, true
ownership is denied. And dissolving the true spirit of ownership
cements the Government Officers into a permanent position...to await
the chance to indulge in further expansion. As with TPOs &
Conservation Orders, the Planning Acts seem to permit officialdom to
muscle in on what is essentially a private matter. This poking around
in other's business seems to extend to members of the public also.
That is, this third party activity is permitted around an intent to
erect a home, office block or factory, & appears to resemble a boxing
or wrestling match where spectators offer advice to the participants
without getting involved with 'the business end of matters'....or
though where planning applications are involved the 'advise maybe of a
compulsory nature. But did someone say we are a democratic Nation?
Well, democracy maybe well & good in electing a government or passing
an Act of Parliament. But surely one should not soil a principle by
excessively employing it to embrace a Communistic type control over
private property.

It is thought that the Listing of Buildings, TPOs & COs have no
justifiable place re: private property. Listing privately owned
residences permit officialdom to harry [or worse] a resident by making
updating to heating & insulation values, or reducing maintenance work
such as fitting plastic windows impossible. See Christchurch
Advertiser 22nd Jan '98] TPOs & CO result in the LA refusing to allow
tree felling, pruning or lopping irrespective of owner's requirement
to prevent loss of safety to life, [eg see Eastbourne Herald Oct 16
1993] limb or property. The various orders under control of officials
even permit officers to cause long term disease to gardens. It took
ten years of continuous effort to obtain permission to clear the cause
of disease in my Hertfordshire property. The diseased garden was
caused by severe sun block from trees protected by a TPO. The public
do not need officials, whether they behave in the manner described or
not, to exercise control over trees on private property. In fact,
they need protection from irresponsible tree planting by whosoever who
show no consideration for another's god given right to daylight
/sunshine!

The public also need long term protection from officialdom who, for
what ever reason, plant trees too close together. A row of mature oak
trees require 50 feet separation...ie a planting density of about
sixteen trees to the acre. Oaks & other forest trees are being planted
six & even four feet apart by officials nation wide. [about 2000 to
the acre] This will cause infestations of insects & fungui which
co- operate & act in isolation to disease neighbouring soil. In the
limit, infestation cannot be controlled even when chemical control is
taken to the extreme that causes human birth deformities. [as suffered
in the USA] The EPIDEMIC of Dutch Elm disease was a good example of
insect/fungus co-operation. As already stated, in the limit food
production becomes impossible also.

Said problems were intensified by mistaken policies adopted at the
Rio Summit earlier this decade. It was thereby agreed that the world

wide human population could expand another two billion or so, to a total of seven to eight billion...providing billions of trees were planted to sop up CO2. But overcrowded trees do not mop up CO2 efficiently because such conditions cause spindly scrub type growth. Overcrowded trees also clash with other human essentials & requirements by damaging foundations to dwellings etc:. Our ancestors knew better. If one wishes to restore, for example, GB to its original jungle type forest state one has to reduce the population first! In any event, population reduction can simply be shown to be a necessity anyway.

If commercial tree densities [as practised on side-lopped fir trees, NOTE one cannot treat oaks in this way] then the trees so planted should be well away from inhabited or farm areas. The quantity of insecticides & fungicides utilised by farmers would then reduce... thereby enhancing the population's health & reducing the National Health cost also. In fact, the density of tree planting should be graded by law according to the distance from specified areas.

Lastly, the practise of planting trees too close together in populated areas or near farmland wastes money on two scores. A tree is claimed to cost £10 to plant. [Source The National Forest] It will cost at least £50 [Writer's estimate] to fell a tree, and in places in the UK where 200 square miles is being planted at approximately 2000 to the acre the long term damage & waste that is being permitted by UK government is inadvisable! Some would say unacceptable. Ultimately, the thinning of the useless scrub being produced will become a necessity. The damaging part of the activity should be halted forthwith!

The matter of population levels is returned to in the interest of completeness. At the time of the Rio summit the World's population stood at about 5 Billion souls. About half of these were contained in India & China who summed about 2 Billion souls. Since the high consumer society exists mainly in the USA, Canada & parts of Western Europe...it follows that over threequarters of the 1992 world population level was not really consuming in global terms. When these populations & their offspring catch up to western standards of living...as they are trying to, & will do...the over plundered Earth will be unable to supply. This exposes the weakness of current policies that try to cope with present levels of population by hounding/pricing the car off the road. This policy is doomed, particularly if it comes to trying the same trick on western Europe with food.

To return to Planning Matters. It is thought there is room for liberating & streamlining the consent requirement for erecting dwellings, shops & office accommodation & factories. One way to achieve this maybe to require Planners to obtain land for each type of building category. The land should be equipped with services like water/gas/electricity set in pre cast concrete trunking. The land could then be sold off at cost for development by individuals, who would be bound by simple rules for traditionally clad buildings. The simple rules may require, for instance, that distance of footings from boundary line would be dependent on height of proposed building. Multistory flats would be built well inside the boundary line...a scheme which would provide space for garages.

Such a scheme may well provide non repetitive building designs & go some way toward creating the charm of an `olde type village'!

Arbitrary power given to Council Officials/workers tends to breed an unhealthy fear of criticising a Council in the minds of the public since a future business or dwelling extension maybe refused by way of reprisal. There is also a `glass barrier' to obtaining signatures for petitions or to hold meetings that involve an MP or residents `get together' to discuss local matters because public halls are barred by contract from allowing so called political meetings. This situation tends to make some Council Employees & Officials officious & also discourages protest! Matters have, according to some petitioners, deteriorated since Councillors have received generous expenses and allowances. The feeling is that we HAVE, GENERALLY, INEFFECTIVE REPRESENTATION LOCALLY, NATIONALLY OR INTERNATIONALLY because our representatives listen mainly to paid officials!

COMMENT

This Report has been presented to provide rationale for suggested Council Tax reductions. The foregoing statement of aim is backed by some 7000 signatures. However, the acceptance of necessary changes may not be instantly approved universally because, for example, some, for whatever reason, like trees crowded together at a density of 2000 per acre. However, most accept the need to be sensible when the needs of Mother Nature are spelt out. Therefore the writer recommends that all the content of this report be properly considered for adoption with careful explanation of the reasoning behind any implementation of advised changes.

In particular, it is thought the Audit Commission, who blamed Council inefficiency on weak Councillors, overpaid management & accuse LA of wasting £1 Billion per year, [see The Times Jan 11th ´95] should investigate the budgetary uncertainties raised in the foregoing text. Particularly, since some associates think that CBC expenditure generally looks to be high for the stated services provided. In addition, there may well be contributory factors in the Audit Commission´s claims of waste in as much as many people without widely based knowledge win power & either ´punch above their weight' with the best of intentions or become bloated with power & push ahead by developing failed policies without giving adequate consideration to the damage/complaints said policies generate. There is thought to be a third possibility, ie that elected persons who find themselves out of their depth may fall under the influence of officials who's main ambition maybe ´Empire Building'.

Remarks made by some petitioners are given -:

Some thought paying the present high levels of Council Taxes is like paying rent to live in your own property... only when renting you get something tangible for your outlay. Other participants asked ´What is the difference between excessive Council Tax demands of LA´s & Protection Racket demands?

November '98

D C TISSINGTON

21 BUCEHAYES CLOSE

HIGHCLIFFE DORSET BH23 5HJ

REF 9

THE PRIME MINISTER/ Ms M MORAN, MP,　　　　　　　　　　3 Mossman Drive,
House of Commons,　　　　　　　　　　　　　　　　　　　Caddington,
London SW1A OAA　　　　　　　　　　　　　　　　　　　Luton Beds

Dear Prime Minister/Ms M Moran,　　　　　　　　　　　　22 December '92
 Further to my stated intent of raising one more issue [see letter dated 28th November '02] before completing Iss 2 of my written constitution ...[.which, in the interests of retaining the soverignty & the expected /due attention of parliament for/ in this Nation of OURS]..... is required to be accepted by Parliament, legally enforcable by the UK Public & is required to override EU LAW & Directives where there is conflict of requirement; whilst tolerating parallel systems.

I refer to my letter to Ms Moran MP, dated 22nd September '02 [the one, there are two of that date which protests to the Beds Police Authority & Parliament [copied to those not previously circulated] about the un-necessary, unacceptable, unsustainable & wasted increases in Local & National taxation & reply from Brian Entwistle from the Office of the Deputy Prime Minister dated 12 Nov '02 which is not acceptable to me ....copy attached.....because it merely restates the detail of said letter dated 22 Sept & the unacceptable consequences in general terms opposed to the particular terms stated in the letter of complaint. CLOSER inspection of the problem presented appears to makes matters more problematic from my point of view! The existing system allows uncontrolled/open ended taxing which 'allows' double charging & other abuses!

I quote[and add to] the last line of the Table of P3 of my report dated Sept '98 Requesting Parliament for Council Tax Reduction [the data employed to construct the graph on P2 showing the rise in Rate/Poll Tax / Council Tax over the life time[1959/'98] of my then Dorset Bungalow when rates [incl sewage] were originally £25 per annum. Generally speaking, all council taxes were approximately equal then, in '98 & now ...ie charges appear orchestrated although spend detail differs from LA to LA. Dorset is used as an example because the detail is published. Increases in household taxes /outgoings over said period ≈3611% versus RPI of +551%. The report was backed with 8000 signatures given to Mr C Chope, OBE MP.

| date | DCC Ex £M | | CBC Ex £M | | Ex £M Police | Sample Band D Bungalow | | | Sewage | Water |
	Gross	Net	Gross	Net		rates	poll tax	Council Tax levy £	£	£
98/9	294	238.8	16.7	3.86	77.4	–	–	759	151	87
99/0	308.5	255.4	17.3	3.979				815		
00/1			17.6	4.077				858		
01/2	371.2	282.37	21.2	4.22	84.58					
02/3	415.0	290.56	21.7	4.87	87.88	–	–	1011	169	114
incr	41%	21.6%	29.9%	26%	13.5%			33%	12.4%	31%
/Ann:	10%	5.3%	7.5%	6.5%	3.5%	–	–	8%	3%	7.8%

Referring to Mr Brian Entwistle's EARLIER letter addressed to me & dated 09 DEC.'98 [attached] The content shows the need for general reform of :LA's, never mind capping, exists, but has not occured.... especially in view of the earliest tax demands about which B Entwistle & the PM were aware of at the time of said letters issue [see B E 's para 1]! At very least there appears to be lack of attention to detail as well as the issue of meaningless words, ie spin. AND CBC's '02 excuse for increases is 'Loss on Int: on balances'.

Standing further back than in para: 2 above, the view I perceive seems to indicate UK Governments [the degree of evidence increases strongly under the last two administrations] is employing the stance of a marauding or invading emperor hell bent on crushing a resentful populace by the time honoured method of ransacking houses affecting life & limb with Trees,TPO's & neighb's from hell , imposing widespread penalising taxes which are then reported by the media as wasted, imposing the deployment of foreign police forces on UK soil [unsupervised at that], fish/food/job losses and imposing overseas customs, systems, directives & law with a view to 'concreating in perpetuity ' the harsh unacceptable conditions listed. I am confident that no UK Government ever won a mandate to behave thus . This paragraph reveals the need for the issued written Constitution to protect us from said abuses of power & which will now be upgraded to issue 2. Sincerely, D C Tissington
CC Home Sec, IDS, Mr Chope, MP, Mr C Kennedy , Mr B Entwistle DETR, Ch Ex CBC & MEDIA

REF 10

**OFFICE OF THE
DEPUTY PRIME MINISTER**

Mr D C Tissington
3 Mossman Drive
Caddington
LUTON
Beds
LU1 4EX

BRIAN ENTWISTLE
Council Tax Policy Team Member

ZONE 5/H5
ELAND HOUSE
BRESSENDEN PLACE
LONDON
SW1E 5DU

Direct line: O20 7944 4186
Fax: 020 7944 4179
GTN: 3533
Brian.entwistle@odpm.gsi.gov.uk

Web site: www.odpm.gov.uk

12 November 2002

Dear Mr Tissington

The copy of the letter of 22 September to your MP, Mrs Moran that you sent to the Prime Minister about council tax reductions has been forwarded to this Department for attention as we are responsible for the council tax. I have been asked to reply.

Levels of council tax may vary from authority to authority for a number of reasons including differences in current and previous spending priorities, management practice, efficiency in delivery of service and collection of revenues owing to them. However, decisions on local taxes are for the local authorities to take, based on the services they want to provide and what local people are willing to pay. Whether and how local taxpayers are consulted is also a matter for individual authorities who are ultimately answerable to their electorate.

You ask if the Government will take steps to stop large council tax increases. Although the Government have reserve capping powers that they can use to control council tax increases that it considers to be excessive, they made clear In their White Paper, Strong Local Leadership - Quality Public Services, that they would only use their powers in exceptional circumstances.

Ministers have carefully considered this year's council tax increases and have concluded that it would not be appropriate for them to use them However, they remain concerned about the level of council tax increases and the willingness of local people to pay them. They have issued guidance to local authorities on best practise in consulting local people about tax and spend decisions and will be looking at how effectively local authorities have engaged their local taxpayers on future council tax increases.

Yours sincerely,

Brian Entwistle

BRIAN ENTWISTLE

Document2

REF 11

DETR
Environment
Transport
Regions

BRIAN ENTWISTLE

LOCAL GOVERNMENT TAXATION

DEPARTMENT OF THE ENVIRONMENT
TRANSPORT AND THE REGIONS

ZONE 5/J2
ELAND HOUSE
BRESSENDEN PLACE
LONDON
SW1E 5DU

Mr D C Tissington
21 Bucehayes Close
Highcliffe
Christchurch
Dorset
BH23 5HJ

TELEPHONE: 0171 890 4186
FAX: 0171 890 4209
GTN CODE: 3533 4186
EMAIL:

09 DECEMBER 1998

Dear Mr Tissington

COUNCIL TAX

The Prime Minister has asked me to thank you for letting him see the copy of your letter of 15 November to your MP, Christopher Chope, enclosing a copy of your report requesting Council Tax reduction. Your letter has been forwarded to this Department for attention as we are responsible for local government finance and I have been asked to reply.

You may wish to be aware that the Government published its Local Government White Paper, "Modern Local Government - In Touch with the People" on 30 July. The paper sets out an agenda for reform and modernisation of local government over ten years or more. The Government's main priorities are to raise standards of council services and making councils more accountable to the people they serve through Best Value, new democratic structures and high ethical standards. I enclose an explanatory leaflet.

On the level of council taxes, part of the increase in council tax has arisen this year because central government support to local government went up by less than the increase in the Government's assessment of total local government revenue expenditure. This reflects the previous Government's stated policy that local tax payers should meet slightly more of the cost of local services. The Government has stuck to existing public expenditure plans and has continued this principle for this financial year. However, the actual level of your council tax depended on the spending decisions of each council.

For the coming financial years, the Government have recently announced the outcome of the Comprehensive Spending Review. This provides a real increase of 2.4/2.2/2.3 per cent over the next three years - an average real increase of 2.3% per year, and a total of £6.59 billion new money over the three years. If councils increase their budgets in line with the SSA increases, council taxes will go up, on average, by 4.5% each year. This compares with increases of 6.2% /6.5% /8.6% over the last 3 years under the previous administration's plans. However, as I mentioned earlier, the actual level of council tax depends on the spending decision of each local authority.

More generally, the Government has said that if local authorities do not deliver prudent budgets or if efficiency and economy fall short of the standards people rightly expect - then Ministers will use reserve powers to limit council tax increases. However, they expect to use the powers rarely.

Yours sincerely

Brian Entwistle.

BRIAN ENTWISTLE

REF 12

1O DOWNING STREET
LONDON SW1A 2AA

From the Correspondence Secretary   7 April 1999

Mr D C Tissington
21 Buce Hayes Close
Highcliffe
CHRISTCHURCH
Dorset
BH23 5HJ

Dear Mr Tissington

    The Prime Minister has asked me to thank you for your recent copy letter.

Yours sincerely

Helen Wyss

MRS H WYSS

1O DOWNING STREET
LONDON SW1A 2AA

From the Correspondence Secretary   16 February 1999

Mr D C Tissington
21 Buce Hayes Close
Highcliffe
CHRISTCHURCH
Dorset
BH23 5HJ

Dear Mr Tissington

    The Prime Minister has asked me to thank you for your
recent copy letter.

Yours sincerely

Helen Wyss

MRS H WYSS

10 DOWNING STREET
LONDON SW1A 2AA

From the Correspondence Secretary   8 February 1999

Mr D C Tissington
21 Buce Hayes Close
Highcliffe
CHRISTCHURCH
Dorset
BH23 5HJ

Dear Mr Tissington

   The Prime Minister has asked me to thank you for your
recent copy letter.

Yours sincerely

MRS H WYSS

REF 13

A NOTE TO THE BRITISH PEOPLE   Nov 29 '04

This note is to sound the alarm bells for GB, ie are GB's affairs being managed to suit T Blair's personal plans? ....There have been a few serious alarms since my interest in UK politics began in the late '50's..But this time, I think the warning is for real & the time for pussy -footing around has gone. However, let me proceed & the reader can then make up his/her own mind.

I am deeply concerned about the behaviour of our local, county , national & 'EU' Governments & the continuing future of OUR Country, GB..

Having documented my observations in some three key documents Ref * / ** / ***....documents that mainly put together the 'gist' of thousands of protest letters that I have sent to polititians, councillors, the media & others over the stated time period. Therefore my claim to have 'seen' most 'of the content of these documents' coming can be shown not to be a matter of idle boasting. The key documents & ref documents are available for inspection/photocopying by appointment to whom so ever. However , to date, not ONE of the many recipients has asked for source of stated disclosures. And hereby hangs a tail...we need changes to Parliamentary & Constitutional proceedures....and a massive change of attitude if this Nation is to maintain its proud traditions: NOT, I hasten to add, the kind Prime Minister Blair seems to be on the point of ' unilaterally elbowing' into existence! I will not list the number of reported 'failings' of the present Government...much of the Media has , & still is, doing a job of sorts in reporting most cases! But there appears to be fundamental gap, ie something missing in their collective reports & it is this I wish to explore.

No MP, Councillor, Minister, Resident's Association Chairman or other public representitive...such as Editors of the media/Press Complaints Commission can walk away from alleged public fraud without investigating the claims & then escape charges of failing their public duty. NB I still await Ms M Moran's report, promised Nov 2001, of SBDC 's Chief Executive's reply re; state of Councils financial practices concerning double charging! Futherto, we know the media is there to make money but with its enormous power comes a DUTY to its Readers & the UK; a duty it is seeming failing to thoroughly discharge!

Council Tax demands are at an all time high....nationally. In the year 1959/1960 the rates on my [now sold] then new Dorset bungalow were £25 per annum..inclusive of Sewage. In the year 1998 the the council tax demand reached £759 & Sewage was a separate charge of £151, a rise of 3611% [makes comparison like for like] in yearly household outgoings against an RPI increase of 551%! These & greralised types of massive increases were brought about by removing council's existing charges to other's budgets & maintaing the charge on the council tax payer...a classic case of double charging & fraud , or so it seems! Other examples included changes to the County Police Budgets, Poll Tax changes etc, Ref **. Pm Tony Blair thanked me for his copy of the report** & promised use of capping powers if LA's did'nt produce prudent budgets in a letter written by Mr B Entwistle dated 12 Dec '98. In 2002, the incremental increase in council tax since '98 reached an additional 33%....with yet another written reply from the PM via Mr B Entwistle dated 12 Nov: 2002 concluding 'it would not be appropriate to use capping powers. In other words woffle, spin & unrestricted increases in tax with no obviouse benefits! The rise in rates, poll tax & council tax is national & is thought to have been achieved by similar methods through-out the land. This is not good enough since all forms of taxation, including council tax, operate on a 'Protection Racket' principle of pay up for a hassle free life ....& as such, MP's should be ever vigilent with the use of a ' Parliamentary protective umbrella' with which to shield otherwise defenceless tax-payers from the unsavoury practices complained of. The media claims that the council tax has increased 60% since New Labour came to power & 2005 reports indicate massive inputs from Whitehall being shovelled in via the back door...with an expected additional 5% increase on each householder for year 2005/2006! All this with an across the board council tax band increase to be announced 'after' the election! Are these extra costs used to create needless jobs to ensure a sympathetic voting base & a diversion from the true aims of New Labour?

In addition, there is the taxation without representation courtesy of the Scottish Assembly [Scotts only are permitted to sit on this Assembly] yet The Whitehall Treasuary coughed up

REF 14

Reference 14 is intensionally missing.... since permission
to reproduce it was not obtained by the Author

REF 15

Her Majesties Opposition Ldrs,
House Of Commons,
London SW1A OAA

3 Mossman Drive,
Caddington,
Luton Beds
LU1 4EX

Mr D Cameron,   12 Feb '07

Thank you for your letter dated 9th Feb '07, not referenced but signed by Ian Pendlington, & the copy of your Sunday Telegraph article dated 4th Feb: 07 'With Reform, Europe can be a Force for Good'.

I don't chastise idealism shown. I don't chastise anybodies ideals ....unless they are formed for personal gain ...as some appear to be! What I am concerned about is the irreversable & fundamental changes being brought about to GB without properly consulting parliament AND equally importantly ...The People of GB. If a prominant Leader, such as PM, has a fundamental & irreversable plan, thats fine. But to act unilaterally without consulting with parliament or the people is treachery! And that impllies a Referendum or a General Election be held!

However, in passing, I will comment on your Aritcle. You will, if you filll the post of PM [& good luck to you in this] be facing the combined forces of some twenty seven political leaders of separate Nations & millions of bureaucrats each with an agenda of their own. Many will wish to keep the gravy train existence, others wish to build their infrastructure on other's funds to maintain elected power! Some are glorified dictators & wish to exercise power. None will yield a inch & the only thing that will prevail is the EU State! Look at the recent example with PM & the French over that continuance of that disgraceful imposition of CAP& its budget. The right course here was for our PM to say reform now or GB will not contribute any more cash to the EU AND we will leave the EU rather than give in. But give in he did. One has to ask why? And with £1.5 million per hour going to Brussels with its non-audited accounts do you wonder there is no money to fund the NHS for example.

If you do not see what is implied here, then you, as PM, will lower this Country of OURS into further decline as most of our past PM's seem to have done. Now perhaps you can see the purpose of ARTICLE 7 CLAUSE 23 in my recent Written Constitution. It also brings me to the point of my opening correspondence with you. I request-:

1 A binding agreement with parliament based on the said Written Constitution ISS 3 dated Jan '07.

2 Request you both assist the British People to obtain a promise from PM of a referendum, which he is reported saying it is not necessary since the business only involves tidying the EU voting system, at the forthcoming EU Summit dated June '07 re the revival of the EU Constitution which will almost certainly remove the remains of GB's Veto & institute a majority voting system .

3 Failure in 2 above requests you & YOUR Lib Dem counterpart to approach Her Majesty Queen Elizebeth II to request that Parliament be dissolved so an Election be held on the matter raised in 2 above.

I will just remind you that failure to implement 2 or 3 above will result in a power loss in which the expense/existence of parliament will no longer be justified because.......

Yours sincerely D.C Tissington

Her Majesty Queen Elizabeth, PM, Ldr Lib Dems, Mr D Davies Shadow Home Sec, Ms M Moran, Media   + FR: 1 sq.

REF 16

The Daily Express,
10 Lower Thames Street,
London EC3R 6EN

Caddington,
Luton Beds
01582 724587

Dear Sir,

12 Feb '07

I refer to the article by L Kellrin in todays Daily Express entitled Is this the end of the road for the Cul de Sac?.

Some of us like our Cul De Sac's & pay for the initial construction access road, which, is then, often abused by non residents long term parking/littering our essential, often unuseable convenience roadway & driving over mowed verges....courtesy of our Councils . The problem is dealt with in my proposed written constitution, Article 10 .

I see Prince Charles & The Home Builders Federation think along with the Government backed Building for Life design scheme all support the end of such estates. But they didn't ask us, who choose to live in these Cul de Sacs! This is typical of the goings on in this Country. But the matter dosn't end there. The group also recommend more densely situated residential homes. AND its a bit rich when some, if not all these 'planners' have never lived in high density housing sites .....especially since the entrance to Highgrove for example could be classed as a low density super & exclusive Cul de Sac!. HD Building sites can make suitable starter homes & retirement housing...but need stringent control of non residents. The matters are raised [from experience] in my written constitutiion, Article 10.
Yours sincerely

D C Tissington

cc Prince Charles & Builders Federation & Builder for Life Design

Please consider this correspondence for your letter column &send a copy to the Chairman of the last two named copy recupiants since I dont know where they operate from. Many thanks

REF 17

Reference 17 is intensionally missing. The Author could not obtain permission to reproduce it without the complication of Royalties.

REF: 18

Local Authority Ombudsman

Mr D Cummings,   3 Mossman Drive,

PO BOX 4471   Caddington,

COVENTRY   CV4 OEH   Luton Beds

                                                  LU1 4EX

Attention of Mr D Cummings,   REF 13 015 320

                                                  28th April 2014
Thank you for your letter dated 23 April 2014 which I find somewhat disturbing.
I am going to be frank but this is not directed at you personally. You are
probabally caught in this mess as much as I am. Having said that you must
realise regardless of the outcome of this letter that matters will continue,if
necessary, until the wrongs have been put right.

I want to expand my observations on parking on housing estates. This problem
goes back to my Highcliffe days which spanned from 1985 till 2000. It is somewhat different here or as I might add, to the rest of the UK. But the reasoned
solutions I am offering will suit all sites.

But first I will give you the facts re: the Caddington property I now live in.
The Plot is 87x14 feet which equals 1218 sq feet An acre equals about 200x200
feet, say 40,000 sq feet. Hence you could get some 33 similar houses to the
acre. There are five similar buildings in this estate & some have slightly
bigger plots while others have somewhat smaller areas.

Since moving here in Dec: 2000, this parking problem in Highcliffe has been
partly addressed but a car parking outside my garage on 29th of April 2014
resulted in a 'speed off' before I could get the ident number of the car
involved.It would have probably have run me down if I had got in front of it,
as intended!

Another parking of two vehicles yesterday, which, like the previous reporting,
but these two were pulled back a bit & I think I could have got out with less
difficulty than with the earlier reporting.[NB Nuisance Parking still occurs &
last occured on 2th January 2015]. The problem with ignoring these
spurious Scouting Parties parkings which would hold me up for a limited time
is that others see the occurance of parking opposite my garage & they occupy
the spot all night or longer and this is completely un-acceptable. So parking
of vehicles ought to be arranged by demolishing some property or properties to
facilitate correct parking.[since councils have failed to allow for correct
amounts of parking in Caddington or else where in the UK] The initial cost of
this should be born by the councils taking from profits made by selling LA
properties at more than costs to the existing owner of Council Housing Estates.
The severe bend in the roadway in Mossman Drive is problematic by preventing
observaton of oncomming traffic when the road is occupied by parked cars &
especially, by larger lorries.

Additionally, Mossman Drive narrows considerably where each side or double
roadside parking occurs which is more or less outside my garage. This occurance
is particularly bad at night as it interferes with my night time exiting of my
garage. I am approaching 90 years of age & the reason I bought this property
since, for example, it might be necessary to get to the hospital. The roadway
at this point is about 15 feet in width so space to manouver & observe
is further restricted, particlarly when big lorrys are parked at this point.

This restriction is partly to blame for vehicles driving on the grass verges &
leaving tyre marks which at times makes the verges look like a ploughed field.

Page 1

In addition, these grass verges are smothered in dandelion plants & the Council
fails to treat these weeds which smother our gardens with weed seed.

I do not think this roadway parking should be allowed, especially since I
bought this property thinking that the council was showing some sign of common
sense. But the bounders didn't activate the condition which prevented roadway
parking. However, the Planning Pemission Document that specified no roadway
parking was to be permitted was part of the planning permission supplied to the
builder of this Estate & was served to me with the deeds of 3 Mossman Drive. I
note that the Council have finally admitted the existance of this document....
but this has not been confirmed by your Department. I request that you ammend
this failour as it is a vital point concerning this complaint. And to make
matters worse, the Caravan Rental Site which is situated behind my garage, &
which is accessed by use of Mossman Drive, has notices proclaiming 'NO PARKING'
except to Caravan Renters...a fact which may be in order. BUT WHAT ABOUT OWNER
OCCUPIERS RIGHTS IN MOSSMAN DRIVE? We have none & this & the ommission needs
correcting because we are wrongly treated BY THE COUNCIL WHO HAS EXCESSIVE
AUTHORITY which your Office seems on the point of enforcing. It is long overdue
that the Government looked at Council Powers which crudely over ride Owner
Occupiers rights. I maintain my view that the Parish Council & the Motoring
Section of the Bedford Council is dismissed from the position that they occupy.

Please note that the Parish Council wrote two favourable letters to the Council
dealing with this problem before failing to correspond further with me, the
applicant. As far as I am aware, the problem stopped with the Parish Council!

And now I have more to say about TREES .....& photographs dealing with Parking
& Trees. But the photographs will have to be sent separately & later....perhaps
by e mail.

Now with regard to FOREST TREES, I understand what you are saying about
restrictions of reporting on FOREST TREES but I do not accept these restrictive
ideals your Department appears to endorse.

There are five mature FOREST TREES existing on the western boundary of Mossman
Drive which the Council accepted before the creation of Mossman Drive or Holy
Farm Close. These trees are threats to the houses foundations in both roadways.
Similarly, problems existed with 60 destroyed saplings in the hedge that exists
about 15 feet from my front door!!! And I think it is time these nutty and
damaging solutions are obliterated from ordinary peoples lives regardless of
Council & some Government Occupiers cracked thoughts on the matter.

Admittedly, these trees do provide Oxygen but they should exist in more distant
& regularly tended forests. What sort of game are these Council & other
Government Departments playing. I would also inform you that the chap who is
supposed to sweep the road only appears when I am actively pushing this
situation.....& perhaps he is understaffed. What I want to know is what does
your Department intend doing to correct the damage being caused by Councils
who cost us, the public, the EARTH, especially when property foundations
are broken up as occured in Caddington village. [It cost 50K Pounds to correct
the
Problem,which may occur again since the trees that caused the problem are sill
flourishing!]

Now the drainage of UK housing sites under discussion are in need of
assistance is shown by the recent floods which occured in England. But some of
my photographs will tend to destroy this false belief that FOREST TREES prevent
floods.....although they may assist in some minor way. The main use of FOREST
TREES is to prevent soil errosion, to house Carbon Dioxide & to generate
Oxygen. As such, they should be kept in regulaly tended forests...sufficiently
well away from farmland & housing estates. Small or NON forest trees should be
used in carefully selected positions to prevent soil errosion on housing
estates & positoned so that sunlight is not unduly blocked. Furthermore, there
are thousands of FOREST TREE seeds lining the roadside gutters on Mossman Drive
[See Photographs] & in peoples gardens, & we need protection from these
occurances.

On this site we have a deep hole....extending some thirty feet or more in
depth to the chalk underlay & the surface water that falls on Mossman Drive is

directed down this 'drain'. And it is effective because there is no sign
of floods to report. I think this system is effective for flood prevenion
throughout the UK.

I would again refer you to a Report issued by BRE entitled LRB Foundations-the
influence of trees on clay soil Ref Digest 298 C1/SIB [16] Wp1 New Edition
April 1999.... which I informed the LA & your Department about in my
communications with you both. AND, I would ask, Why have you & the Council
completely failed to mention this Report which provides the 'safe' distance
between listed FOREST TREES & private houses concerning ROOTS on clay sub-
soils? And why did you & the Council fail to mention this Document in your
letters addressed to me. The failure looks to me as though the matter was
being avoided for some reason ....perhaps to obscure faulty thoughts.

Since my MP, Mr G Shuker, fails to correspond with me for reasons unknown
[Its 15 months since I heard from him]...I will have to make other arrangements
to get these matters sorted if this matter is out 'of touch' for your
Organisation But I ask what is the use of Referees who cannot or will not
deal with genuine wrongs. Perhaps the Prime Minister will act to sort this
matter out if necessary due to faults in Personale or Systems. I am also
unable to get meaningful attention from my MP regarding the sale of my
Caribbean Property ....so something ought to be done to correct this inability.

Regards

Daniel Tissington

CC To Prime Minister Mr G Shuker MP & Leader of the UKIP.

NB This letter has been corrected by correction or obliteration of some words
in order to correct spelling or grammer. But the meaning of the script has
not been altered. The problem occured due to the Ombudsman giving a short time
limit for me to answer .....a bit much when one considers the problem has been
addressed over a ten year period!

The tallest building on the left show pictures of the garages allotted to No 1 & No 3 [my property] Mossman Drive.
Shows author's garage with view of oncoming traffic entering Mossman Drive blocked.

View of my garage taken from bedroom window.
Author's garage with exiting view of other traffic leaving Mossman Drive blocked.

Irresponsible parking outside Author's garage.

Picture shows multitude of Forest Tree Seeds in the gutter of Mossman Drive.

Photo shows Forest Trees on the boarder of Mossman Drive & Holly Farm which are too close to buildings in both roads…see Ref 6.

Irresponsible parking blocking view of incoming & outgoing traffic when viewed from Writers garage exit.

Shows width of Mossman Drive just south of Writer's garage which is 15 feet.

Shows type of parking which obstructs writer's view when leaving garage forecourt.

Shows large van parked right outside author's garage.

More blockage of view of oncoming traffic when leaving Authors garage.